User Interface Management Systems:
Models and Algorithms

The Morgan Kaufmann Series in Computer Graphics and Geometric Modeling

Series Editor, Brian A. Barsky (University of California at Berkeley)

Richard H. Bartels, John C. Beatty, and Brian A. Barsky
An Introduction to Splines for Use in Computer Graphics and Geometric Modeling (1987)

Christoph M. Hoffmann
Geometric and Solid Modeling: An Introduction (1989)

Norman I. Badler, Brian A. Barsky, and David Zeltzer, editors
Making Them Move: Mechanics, Control, and Animation of Articulated Figures (1991, book and videotape)

Dan R. Olsen, Jr.
User Interface Management Systems (1992)

Andrew S. Glassner
Ray Tracing: Theory and Practice (1992)

Julian Gomez, David Zeltzer, et al.
Computer Animation: Principles and Practice (1992, book and videotape)

Brian Wyvill and Jules Bloomenthal, editors
Implicit Surfaces: Theory and Application in Computer Graphics (1992)

User Interface Management Systems:
Models and Algorithms

Dan R. Olsen, Jr.

Morgan Kaufmann Publishers
San Mateo, California

Sponsoring Editor: Michael B. Morgan

Production Editor: Yonie Overton

Cover Designer: Our House Design Group

Cover Illustrator: Christine Gralapp

Text Designer: Susan Sheldrake

Compositor/Indexer: S.M. Sheldrake Graphic Design

Copyeditor: Siân Jarman

Proofreaders: Lynn Meinhardt, Gary Morris

Morgan Kaufmann Publishers, Inc.
Editorial Office:
2929 Campus Drive, Suite 260
San Mateo, CA 94403

95 94 93 92   5 4 3 2 1

Library of Congress Cataloging-in-Publication Data is available for this book.

To Stephanie, Melanie, Dan, Kimberly, Stephen, Kari, Nathan, Kristen, and their mother Vickie, who all bring such joy to me, and to the God who has made this and so many other good things possible in my life.

Acknowledgements

The text of this book has very much benefited from the hours of reading, editing, questioning, and correcting done by Douglas Campbell.

This work and the decade of research behind it would not have been possible without the backing of Tom Harris. He has faithfully supported this work from long before it became popular.

I am also grateful for the encouragement and support of Bill Hays: a teacher, department chairman, and friend.

Lastly, I would like to thank all of my many colleagues in the user interface research community. Much of this book reflects their professional work but more than that I am grateful for the wonderful people that they are and the joy that they are to associate and work with.

Dan R. Olsen, Jr.
Brigham Young University

Contents

1. Introduction 1

Computer Graphics and the User Interface 1
The Nature and Evolution of UIMSs 2
The Process..6
Personnel Roles in User Interface Development 8
Purposes for UIMSs..10
Overview of the Book...11

2. UIMS Architectures 15

Lexical Issues..16
Semantics..23
Data Display 31
Dialog Manager 32
An Example 34
Summary...35

3. State Machine UIMSs 37

Simple State Machines 37
Recursive State Machines 41
Semantic Attributes..48
Pervasive States 52
Semantic Control 55
Summary of State Machine Approaches........................57

4. Grammar UIMSs **59**

Basic Parse Algorithm 59
Typed Picking...64
Rub Out..66
Recursive Descent Generation 66
Extended Grammars 71
Summary of Grammar UIMSs 72

5. Event-based UIMSs..............................**73**

MENULAY 73
Window Systems 75
Object-oriented Event Systems 79
HyperCard 84
Summary of Event Handling....................................89

6. Production Systems **91**

Event Response Language 93
Propositional Production Systems............................97
Production Systems and other Event Handling Models............113
Summary 113

7. Dialog Trees **115**

Basic Algorithm..116
Layered Menus and Defaults 118
Reenter 121
Semantic Control of the Dialog 122
Full Dialog Tree Traversal Algorithm 122
Summary 127

8. Language UIMS Models.......................**129**

EZWin...129
MIKE...134
Mickey 146

9.   Constraint Systems for Visual Presentation **153**

Overview of Constraint Systems 154
User Interface Visual Presentations 167
Summary 180

10.   Editing Dialog Models **183**

Motivation for Data-based UIMS Models 184
Cousin 184
Editing Templates 185
Architecture of Editing Templates 187
ITS 188
Sushi 193
Summary 201

11.   Interface Quality **203**

Predictive Analysis 203
Measurement of Implemented Interfaces 206
Transforming Interface Designs 214
Summary 217

1.
Introduction

The history of computing has been one of harnessing the power of a machine to meet the needs of man. This process is seen most powerfully in the development of graphical human-computer interfaces. A major impediment to this harnessing process, however, has been the cost of developing software that tames the technology for human use and interacts in human rather than in machine terms.

In order to build quality user interfaces for a variety of graphical applications the notion of a User Interface Management System (UIMS) has been developed. This field of research has not reached maturity and only a handful of UIMSs have become commercial products. Most UIMSs have not left the laboratories where they were born. There is, however, a widening interest in applying this technology.

This book presents a wide range of research that has been done on UIMSs. The focus of the book will be on UIMS architectures and implementations. UIMSs are primarily aimed at graphical user interfaces and there will be little or no discussion of traditional textual user interfaces.

Computer Graphics and the User Interface

Historically, user interface issues have developed in tandem with the growth of computer graphics. With the advent of Sketchpad[1] the potential for computer graphics to provide an interactive medium was recognized. The user interface to Sketchpad, a bank of toggle switches, seems rather primitive today. Even in those early days researchers were building tools to aid in developing user interfaces. The earliest system which might be called a UIMS was Newman's Reaction Handler[2] which used the basic state machine as its model.

For many years the handling of graphical input was virtually ignored, as researchers struggled with questions of geometry, optics, lighting, and modeling of virtual worlds. Simultaneously, computer graphics became steadily cheaper and more widely available. Early storage-tube display technology (which the majority of users had available to them) was not amenable to highly interactive programs. Textual interfaces with some informational pictures were the rule. The vector refresh technology was highly interactive but very expensive and thus not widely available. The vector refresh applications were all carefully handcrafted to take advantage of the special graphics hardware and display devices of each machine.

The major discussions concerning input during this period could be summarized by the differentiation between sampled and event devices, and the notion that inputs should not be directly linked to their output echoes. The separation of input and output allowed a variety of echoing and interactive techniques to be programmed.[3] These two concepts carried user input research in the graphics community up to the point of the CORE[4] and GKS[5] graphics standards.

With the advent of microprocessors and semiconductor memory the nature of computer graphics changed entirely. Raster displays came to dominate the marketplace; almost every personal computer has some graphics capability. With the processor intimately linked with the graphics display in low cost workstations the notion of a quality user interface became economically feasible and, soon, very important. It was during this period that UIMS research began to flourish. The computer graphics community was undergoing a radical transformation but the basic tenets of separation of input and output would remain, and influence UIMS development for many years to come.

The Nature and Evolution of UIMSs

UIMS research focused around three workshops sponsored by the ACM (Association for Computing Machinery), EUROGRAPHICS, and IFIPS. These workshops brought together a wide range of researchers, set much of the conceptual terminology, and defined the problems and challenges facing UIMS researchers.

Seattle

The first workshop was held in Seattle in 1982.[6] At this point only a handful of UIMSs had been built or published and the term User Interface Management System had not come into wide usage. The major conclusions of this workshop were:

1. The user interface implementation should be separated from the application code and be implemented using specialized programming tools.
2. Interactive applications should have external rather than internal control. The user interface and its supporting software would control the flow of the application (external control) rather than the application code itself (internal control).
3. Tools should be developed to assist user interface developers who are not necessarily programmers.
4. User interfaces should be specified using a separate dialog description tailored specifically for user interface design rather than programmed in a general purpose language.

These points represented a radical departure from normal development of graphical user interfaces, where interactive input was handled by the application calling subroutines from a library.

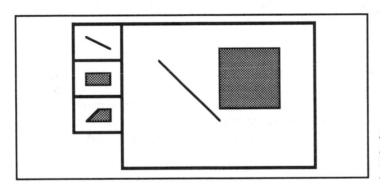

Fig. 1:1

Sample
Drawing
Application

To illustrate these points take the sample drawing application shown above. Traditional user interface techniques would consist of the following kinds of activities.

- Write code to draw each of the icons on the screen
- Write code to draw each of the objects in the draw window
- Write dialog handling code which:

1. gets a mouse input and decides which icon was selected
2. based on the icon selected, gets inputs for the object to be drawn
3. draws the object and adds it to the list of objects maintained by the application.

There are several problems with this strategy. The first is that icons, and other pictorial information, must be specified in code rather than by drawing. This is painful to do, even for programmers, and eliminates the possibility of a graphics artist participating in the icon design. An additional problem is that the dialog is too rigid. If, in the middle of drawing a rectangle, the user wants to draw a polygon instead, the rectangle must be completed and deleted, and only then can the polygon be drawn. Allowing a more flexible dialog requires a lot of special code from the programmer.

If the icon images are not embedded in the code, but are placed in a separate dialog specification, then tools can be written that allow either programmers or graphic artists to draw rather than code the appearance of the icons. This is the essence of points 1 and 3 from the Seattle workshop. If the dialog specification is also pulled out of the code, more powerful control models can be created that allow users to freely exit dialog fragments and start something new. This is the essence of point 2, about external and internal control. The dialog required for this draw program is rather simple and does not require a great deal of understanding. The specification of more complicated dialogs with hundreds of commands and objects is what drives point 4.

Seeheim

The second workshop was held in Seeheim, Germany in 1983.[7] By this time a number of UIMSs had been built and research centers had been working hard on the UIMS problem. The most widely known contribution from this workshop was the Seeheim model for UIMS architectures. This model reflected the architectures of many of the existing UIMSs.

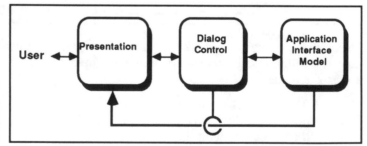

Fig. 1:2
*Seeheim
Model
for UIMS
Architecture*

The Seeheim architecture calls for three UIMS components. The primary component is the *dialog control* which receives inputs, determines what should be done about them, and requests services from the application. The application code is accessed via some *application interface model,* which is also called the *semantic interface.* The *presentation* consisted of all those issues that control the visual appearance and physical device selection of the actual interface.

This model called for graphical output of application data to be generated by the application under the control of the dialog manager, with the presentation controlling the external appearance. The notion of the dialog control having an influence over the presentation of application data is signified in the diagram by the small circle around the path from the application interface to the presentation. This data display facet of the model has not been fully realized in any UIMS.

In our example drawing application, the images of the icons would be part of the presentation. The drawing of the lines, rectangles, and polygons in the draw area would be done by the application, through the presentation. The presentation, for example, would know where the draw area is actually located relative to the icons. The dialog control might influence this drawing by making sure that the currently selected object is highlighted. In this application it is the dialog control's responsibility to know that after selecting the rectangle icon, any mouse activity in the draw area should be used to draw the desired rectangle. The application interface model might simply be a set of commands such as:

```
DrawLine(X1,Y1,X2,Y2)
DrawRect(X1,Y1,X2,Y2)
StartPoly(X,Y)
AddPolyPoint(X,Y)
EndPoly()
```

The dialog control would then receive the mouse inputs and decide which of the application commands should be called up and what arguments they should receive.

Seattle Revisited

The third workshop was again held in Seattle, in 1986.[8] The primary results of this meeting were:

- The UIMS tools and interface descriptions should support the process of user interface design rather than simply its implementation. This includes all of the issues from software engineering, which have rather unique problems when applied to user interface development.
- Earlier UIMS architectures, including the Seeheim model, suffered serious problems in facing the demands of direct manipulation interfaces. Most of these problems were the result of the separation of input from output, which had been inherited from earlier graphics research and had permeated many UIMS developments.

These workshops served only as focal points for a range of research that began well before 1982 and which is still emerging. It is important to note that as research has progressed, the emphasis has expanded beyond the narrow questions of quick and easy implementation of the interface, to encompass the entire user interface design process.

The Process

In order to design a good UIMS one must first consider the nature of the development process that an interactive application goes through. In many ways this is similar to the standard approaches from software engineering, but there are several unique characteristics of graphical user interfaces that need consideration; particularly in light of the design and implementation tools that should be incorporated into the UIMS.

The 1986 Seattle workshop identified the following relevant software engineering phases:

- requirements
- specification and design
- implementation
- testing
- maintenance

The requirements phase is pretty much standard, although some human factors practitioners have advocated the inclusion of usability criteria in the requirements[9] which specify measurable productivity, error rate, and learnability goals for the end product. The role of the UIMS in meeting usability requirements will be discussed in the chapter on interface evaluation *(Chapter 11)*.

The specification and design phase actually has several parts which can be broken down along the lines of the Seeheim model. The first and most critical part is the design of the application's functionality. Functionality is characterized by specifying the application/UIMS interface. There are a number of forms that the application interface and its specification might take, some of which directly support functional design of the interface and other forms which simply support the implementation. The variety of semantic interface models will be discussed in Chapter 2.

Once the functional design of the interface is complete, proceeding sequentially through presentation design and dialog design and then on to implementation and testing is not appropriate for user interface design. At present the only known method for creating a quality user interface design is an iterative process of creating a design, implementing it, testing it with users, and modifying it. In addition, the specification of presentation and dialog are heavily intertwined, since the dialog design is controlled by the presentation of the application data and it in turn controls the kinds of icons, dialog boxes, and other presentational items that are required. Compare, for example, the Macintosh Finder with the UNIX command line. This change in presentation of the information radically affects the nature of the dialog. The key issue for the design of user interfaces is flexibility in the tools. The tools must support rapid modification and testing of a design to facilitate convergence to an acceptable user interface.

The iterative nature of user interface design poses several challenges to UIMS developers. The first of these is to create models for dialog and presentation descriptions. Such descriptions should be easily modified and quickly turned into working implementations that can be tested. This includes tools both for editing the dialog specification and for drawing, or otherwise designing, the external presentation of the interface. The challenge of designing elegant dialog and presentation models has been the driving force in most UIMS development.

A second challenge is to be able to evaluate a design. The most attractive approaches are predictive evaluation tools which analyze the dialog specification to identify design weaknesses before implementation. This approach is particularly attractive due to the fact that most UIMSs are characterized by a machine-readable dialog specification which could, potentially, be analyzed.

A third challenge is to provide support tools to evaluate the performance of actual working user interfaces and to indicate where problems exist and where changes should be made. A particularly ambitious goal is not only to identify where problems in the interface design or implementation exist but also to suggest specific remedies or otherwise directly aid in selecting remedies for problems that have been detected.

Few UIMSs have addressed the maintenance and functional testing problem. Many software development environments provide tools for managing test sets and evaluating output. These tools allow regression tests to be created, maintained, and semiautomatically applied to new versions of the software. In an interactive graphics application, test set maintenance is much more difficult. There is no source file that can be applied as the test input, and the output is primarily defined in terms of what appears on the screen. There is a potential for UIMS-based tools to provide assistance here, because of their control of all user inputs. As yet, however, no UIMSs have attacked this problem.

Personnel Roles in User Interface Development

We have reviewed the process of creating graphical interfaces and the tools that are required to support these processes. Let us now look at the users of these tools. A UIMS is itself a piece of software and in many cases is an interactive graphical application in its own right. As such it is important to consider its user community in deciding exactly what the nature of these tools should be and how best such tools might serve their constituents. Several roles have been defined as being involved in the user interface development process.[10] These roles may be filled by various individual specialists or several may be shared by one person. They are not presented as an organizational guideline but rather to characterize the needs that tools must fill and the skills of those using the tools. One of the main goals of UIMS development is to provide tools that allow direct involvement of all participants in the interface design process. In particular, it is desirable for each participant to work directly with the appropriate design tool without having to work indirectly through a programmer in order to affect the design.

End Users

The end users are the only community whose satisfaction really matters for any application development. Although end users are familiar with their own job, its problems, their goals, and the functionality they need, they do not always have a good idea of how their user interfaces should function. They are much better at indicating what they do not like, or what is not working well, than they are at specifying a new approach. These attributes of an end user lead to the iterative design process described above, where a working user interface or simulation is provided as early as possible so that the end user can comment on it. It is of great benefit to be able to make immediate changes to the interface via the UIMS tools rather than referring the problem to programmers for future corrections.

Application Analyst

An application analyst acts as the bridge between the end user and the user interface designer. The application analyst must define the functionality of the user interface and ensure that it has been provided for. This role requires an understanding of the application domain, the end user's needs, and what is and is not feasible for computers to do. In general, this role is filled by a knowledgeable end user rather than by a programmer. The role is not to create the interface but to define what it should do. Tools to support this role include clear, easily learned functional definitions for user interfaces.

Dialog Author

The dialog author is the primary designer of the user interface. Persons filling this role are responsible for creating the metaphors of the "virtual world" that end users are to work in. Such individuals must have:

- a broad exposure to a variety of user interface styles,
- a clear understanding of the trade-offs in selecting various user interface approaches,
- a knowledge of a variety of interactive techniques and of their strengths and weaknesses in various situations,
- and a knowledge of how such techniques interact with each other.

The dialog author generally accepts the desired functionality of the interface as a given and attempts to create an effective facade that allows end users to exploit that functionality. The primary tool of the dialog author is the dialog description, where the behavior of the interface in response to various user inputs is defined. The role of dialog author is one of specifying the interface and not one of programming. In many cases good dialog authors are average to poor programmers primarily because their expertise and interests lie in other areas.

Graphics Designer

The graphics designer creates the visual appearance of the user interface. This includes icon design and screen layout as well as color, typeface, and pattern selection. The skills brought to this task are ones of creating a pleasing and informative display of the "virtual world." The natural medium for graphics designers is to draw how the interface should appear. Textual specification languages, including programming languages, are *ineffective* tools for this role.

Applications Programmer

The applications programmer must program the application functionality. They must have a general knowledge of the application domain and should be knowledgeable about the data structures, algorithms, and support services that this domain requires. In general they are poor graphics designers, being accustomed to highly stylized specification languages rather than the clear visual forms that end users of graphical interfaces require. They are generally not well acquainted with a wide range of user interface styles nor with the human factors implications of the various styles. Their primary need is a good programming language and a clearly understood interface to the UIMS.

User Interface Evaluator

A user interface evaluator must evaluate a user interface's performance relative to the criteria set for it. In many cases such an evaluation consists of nothing more than letting a group of people use the system and then recording their complaints. Many problems such as poor productivity, high error rates, or slow learning are not identified by such coarse-grained approaches. Additional tools are required for measuring performance, analyzing dialog descriptions to identify where the problems are, and to suggest remedies. Such analysis and measurement tools rely heavily on the concept of a separate dialog description from which the implementation is generated.

Purposes for UIMSs

In designing User Interface Management Systems a variety of goals have been espoused. The primary goal has always been to reduce the amount of effort required to create a new user interface. Development productivity was the original impetus for UIMS research. As research has progressed, however, a number of other goals have been identified.

A major goal is the reliability of the resulting interface. Unreliable code is a product of programmers making mistakes in the implementation. People do not generally excel in exhaustively considering all of the possibilities. Exhaustive analysis, however, is relatively easy for a code generator. In most UIMSs a great deal of the user interface code is either part of a standard library of code or is automatically generated by the UIMS tools. The less code generated by hand, the fewer cases of erroneous behavior there will be. This assumes that the dialog description is clear and straightforward to the developers and does not introduce complexities of its own.

A major attribute of good user interfaces is consistency. In a consistent interface similar actions are expressed in similar ways. The advent of the Apple Macintosh has greatly strengthened the argument for interface consistency between applications. Some UIMSs impose a particular style on the interface or a particular set of techniques. This may limit the range of user interfaces that the UIMS can create, but the desired interface consistency is an automatic by-product of using the UIMS rather than a requirement to be enforced.

The need for direct support of the user interface development process and the personnel involved has been discussed earlier. Attempting to support the needs and skills involved in interface design has been a primary cause of the variety of UIMS models that have been developed. A review of the personnel roles defined above shows that a programming language is unacceptable as a tool for most of the players. The notion of directly supporting the various participants in user interface design leads one to the set of specialized development tools found in a UIMS.

A final purpose for UIMS development is to provide interactive facilities that are difficult to provide in hand-generated code. Features such as macros by example or interface usage measurements depend heavily on a UIMS implementation. Many features are so costly to develop that unless the costs are amortized over a great many applications developed with the UIMS, they become impractical. Other facilities, by their very nature, depend upon the separate machine-readable dialog description found in all true UIMSs.

Overview of the Book

The primary aim of this book is to present the state of the art in UIMS development. At present there are few commercial UIMSs to choose from. Many practitioners must build their own UIMS, or portions of it. Therefore, emphasis will be placed on the nature of the models that control each UIMS, the strengths and weaknesses of the models, and on the underlying algorithms that each model uses to control the human-computer dialog.

This book will not devote a lot of space to human factors issues. There are already a number of books on the human factors of interface design. The emphasis here is on the software architecture of the user interface. The needs of human factors experts themselves must, however, be considered in the UIMS design as has already been discussed, and these issues will be addressed.

Chapter 2 will discuss the general architecture used in most UIMSs and will define a number of terms that are used in the literature. In particular, the issues of how a UIMS interfaces with the application are discussed, since these are general across most UIMS models. The semantic interface is of most interest to application programmers, dialog authors, and application analysts.

Following the architecture discussion several chapters are devoted to various models for specifying interactive dialogs in terms of the inputs received from the user. The chapters on state machine, grammar, event models, and production systems describe UIMS strategies that focus on how the user inputs are to be handled and translated into semantic actions from the application domain. The state machine and grammar models are designed primarily with the dialog author in mind. They provide little support for visual presentation aspects of the interface or for how the application functionality should be organized. Some of the event models, however, are based on drawing metaphors that directly support the role of graphics designer.

The chapters on dialog trees and language models describe UIMS approaches that focus more on what the interface is to accomplish and less on how the individual events are handled. (This is also true of the chapter on editing models.) These models are strongly influenced by the desired functionality of the interface and thus provide much better support for the application analyst. Many of these models bypass the dialog specification entirely and thus require little direct involvement from a dialog author.

The chapter on constraint systems and visual presentations discusses techniques for connecting visual images to the underlying semantics and to the inputs. The constraint systems themselves are beyond the abilities of most graphics designers. This chapter does, however, discuss tools for interactively laying out the visual interface, with the constraint specification being handled automatically.

The chapter on editing models takes the point of view that most user interface activity is concerned with browsing through or editing information. Based on this point of view several systems bridge the application-to-interface gap by generating editors automatically. The notion of editing also ties together the visual presentation of information and the interactive inputs to manipulate it. This chapter places strong emphasis on the application analyst and the graphics and dialog designers.

The final chapter discusses techniques for supporting the evaluation of user interfaces. Since a UIMS has control of all of the interactive I/O (input/output) in the user interface, there are a number of support functions that can ease the burden of evaluating the quality of an interface. The fact that a UIMS has a separate dialog specification also opens up the possibility of automatically analyzing the interface specification. All of these techniques are intended to support the role of dialog evaluator.

References

1 Sutherland, I.E. *Sketchpad: A Man-Machine Graphical Communication System.* **SJCC.** Baltimore, MD: Spartan Books, 1963.

2 Newman, W. *A System for Interactive Graphical Programming.* **SJCC.** Washington, DC: Thompson Books, 1968, 47-54.

3 Guedj, R.J. and others (eds.). **Workshop IFIP on Methodology of Interaction.** Seillac, France: North-Holland, May 1979.

4 *Status Report of the Graphic Standards Planning Committee.* **Computer Graphics** 13(3), August 1979.

5 *Graphical Kernel System.* **Computer Graphics,** Special GKS Issue, Feburary 1984.

6 Thomas, J.J. and G. Hamlin. *Graphical Input Interaction Technique (GIIT): Workshop Summary.* **Computer Graphics** 17(1): 5-68, January 1983.

7 Pfaff, G.E. (ed.). **User Interface Management Systems.** Heidelberg: Springer-Verlag, 1985.

8 *ACM SIGGRAPH Workshop on Software Tools for User Interface Management.* **Computer Graphics** 21(2): 71-150, April 1987.

9 Whiteside, J., J. Bennett, and K. Holtzblatt. *Usability Engineering: Our Experience and Evolution.* **Handbook of Human-Computer Interaction,** M. Helander (ed.). Amsterdam: North-Holland, 1988.

10 Olsen, D., W. Buxton, R. Ehrich, D. Kasik, J. Rhyne, and J. Sibert. *A Context for User Interface Management.* **IEEE Computer Graphics and Applications** 4(12): 33-42, December 1984.

2.
UIMS Architectures

Early researchers decomposed the structure of an interactive program into lexical, syntactic, and semantic levels.[1] This decomposition is derived from research in language processing and compiler construction. To some extent this decomposition is found in the Seeheim model, with the lexical considerations lying inside the presentation. This notion of three levels has pervaded UIMS research for a number of years. Many UIMSs have this structure in their actual software architecture. With the rising interest in direct manipulation interfaces, however, the model presented here is more of a subdivision of the issues of user interface construction rather than a literal software architecture.

The following diagram shows the logical architecture that we will use in discussing most UIMSs.

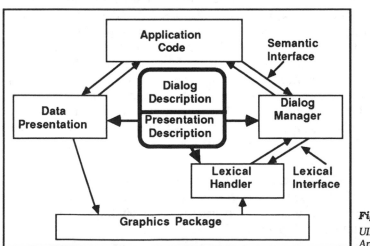

Fig. 2:1
UIMS
Architecture

The lexical level is encompassed by the Lexical Handler, the input portion of the Graphics Package, and the lexical specifications in the Presentation Description. The syntactic level is found in the Dialog Manager and the Dialog Description. The semantic level consists of the Application itself and the Semantic Interface. Some authors have attempted to lump the Data Presentation component into the syntactic level by means of a vague and as yet unimplemented concept of output syntax. In reality it is not accounted for at all in the Lexical/Syntactic/Semantic model. This model had its basis in language processing and in the days when input was strictly segregated from output.

None of the UIMS models that we will discuss will seriously constrain the graphics package they are built on top of. It is assumed that the actual drawing of images on the screen and the handling of physical inputs will be done by some graphics package. UIMSs have been built on both CORE[2] and GKS.[3] However, most current UIMS work is being done on top of X-Windows. For the most part we will ignore the characteristics of the graphics device, leaving these considerations to the graphics package. The architectural discussion will center around the handling of lexical level input, interfacing with the application semantics, the visual presentation, and management of the interactive dialog.

Lexical Issues

The lexical level of a user interface's input is generally viewed as a set of logical input devices. A logical device is characterized by its software interface and, in particular, by an identification of the device and the type of value that it returns. A physical device is an actual piece of hardware. One of the pieces of information that must exist in the presentation description is a mapping of the physical to the logical devices. For example, the logical device "Delete" might be mapped to the physical key "F1" as part of a presentation description. In this case the logical device is characterized by its identifier and the fact that it has no value. A second example would be a logical device "ScrollX" which is mapped to a physical device that is knob number 4. ScrollX is a logical device that can be sampled for a Real value.

One of the characteristics of the lexical level is that it attempts to isolate the logical or software view of a device from its actual physical implementation by means of the logical/physical bindings found in the lexical presentation description.

In many cases a physical device does not exist for a given logical device. For example, most personal computers do not have knobs. In this case a logical device can be implemented as a virtual device. A virtual device is a software simulation of a logical device. In the Apple Macintosh software the logical device ScrollX is simulated by a scroll bar drawn across the bottom of a window. Logically the movement of a scroll bar's thumb is the same as turning a knob, and the remainder of the software need only know about the logical concept of ScrollX and can be implemented independently of the use of a physical or virtual implementation. Another example of a virtual device is the substitution of an icon for a physical button. The lexical level is responsible for the management of the menu. The presentation description contains the information for laying out the menu but the remainder of the software knows only about the logical button.

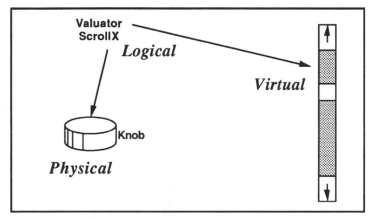

Fig. 2:2

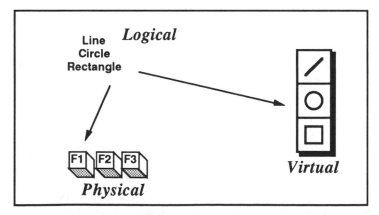

Fig. 2:3

Early researchers asserted that any physical device could be simulated by a virtual device.[1,4] This lead to the CORE and GKS concepts of standard sets of logical devices which would either be mapped to physical devices or simulated as virtual devices. This provided some measure of device independence and portability. It was soon noted that in many cases the substitution of a virtual simulation for a given input device would significantly change the usability of the user interface. Simply having the graphics package make such substitutions automatically creates user interface problems. Such substitution by dialog authors, however, by modifying the presentation description, is a useful technique in many situations.

Logical Device Properties

The Lexical Handler interfaces primarily with the Graphics Package and the Dialog Manager. The interface to the graphics package is determined by the package itself and needs no further discussion. The interface between the Dialog Manager and the Lexical Handler, however, is of interest. Several properties of logical devices were identified as part of the GKS design process. Most of these are of interest in discussing the Dialog Manager/Lexical Handler interface.

Every logical device has a measure and/or a trigger.[5] A device's measure is simply its current value. For example, the measure of a scroll bar or knob is its Real value. The measure of a mouse is its current location. A trigger is an event that indicates that the device's measure is now important to the software. For example, the trigger on a mouse might be one or any of the buttons on the mouse. The measure of a keyboard would be the ASCII value of the key that was struck and the trigger would be the depression of one of the keys.

In early graphics packages, devices were classified as either event or sampled. An event device is one for which the user specifies the time that the device's measure becomes significant. For instance, keyboards and buttons were classified as event devices. Sampled devices are ones where the software determines when the measure is important and asks the graphics package for the current value. This strict separation between event and sampled devices proved unworkable. For example, if a key is held down some software systems want to repeat the character. This would mean that the keyboard would need to be sampled to see if the key is still being held down. On the other hand, we frequently do not want to sample the mouse continuously but rather we wait for its button to be pressed before paying attention to the mouse. As we will see later, many current systems treat all devices as event devices in order to simplify the software structure.

For most graphical devices and for most applications there are not enough physical devices to allow a one to one mapping between physical and logical devices. In some contexts, for example, the key "F1" might be the logical device "DeleteLine" and in another context "F1" might be bound to "DeleteReference." There are two ways of demultiplexing, the correct use of a physical device. The first is temporal demultiplexing, where the current context of the user interface is used to determine the physical/logical binding. The second is spatial demultiplexing, which is also widely used, where the location of a pointing device like a mouse is used to make the physical/logical binding. An example of temporal demultiplexing is illustrated by mapping "F1" to "DeleteLine" when in text edit mode, and to "DeleteReference" when in footnote mode. A example of spatial demultiplexing is when clicking on the Circle icon maps the mouse location to the logical device ""DrawCircle," while clicking on the Rectangle icon maps the mouse location to the logical device "DrawRect."

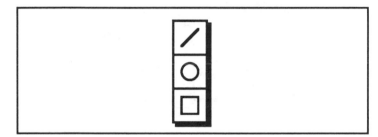

Fig. 2:4

The temporal demultiplexing of physical/logical device bindings is handled by the notions of acquire, release, and context. When one acquires a logical device all of its physical resources are bound to the logical device. This is particularly important in the case of virtual devices that are simulated on the screen. When a menu device, for example, is acquired, it is displayed on the screen or otherwise attached to the lexical handler's menu mechanism. When a scroll bar is acquired it is drawn on the screen. When one releases a device the physical resources are removed from the logical device. In the case of simulated devices they are removed from the screen. This definition means that two logical devices which share physical resources cannot be acquired simultaneously. A context is a set of acquired logical devices. In general, when one enters a context all logical devices not in the set are released and all logical devices in the set are acquired. In a later discussion the output issues associated with a context such as screen layouts, active windows, etc., will be discussed. For now, however, we will consider a context to be simply the list of acquired devices.

A logical device may be acquired because it is part of the current context but it may not be currently enabled. A logical device is enabled when its input is currently acceptable to the application. For example, the menu item "Save" might be disabled until some change has been made in a file. It should appear in the menu because it is acquired and forms part of the screen layout, but it should not be accepted until its meaning is legal. A logical device can therefore be enabled and disabled. When a device is released it is automatically disabled since it no longer has any physical resources. Related to the notion of enabled devices is a device's prompt. The prompt is an indication to the user that the device is currently available for input and some indication of what information is required. On the Apple Macintosh the prompt for scroll bars is a gray background. The following figures show scroll bars unacquired, disabled, and enabled.

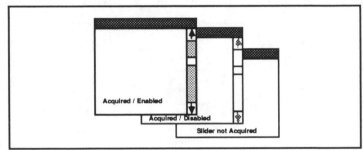

Fig. 2:5
Scroll Bars

Finally, a device should possess an echo and an acknowledge. The echo is an indication of the current value of the device's measure. For example, the echo of the mouse is the cursor on the screen. The echo in a menu is the highlighting of the item currently under the cursor. The

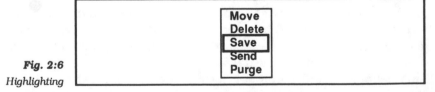

Fig. 2:6
Highlighting

acknowledge of a device is some indication that the input has been accepted. A menu item may flash or some other indicator may occur. We will not consider the acknowledge further since it is handled within the lexical handler and is not a property of the Lexical/Dialog interface.

Lexical/Dialog Interface

A key to our future discussion of dialogs is the interface between the Dialog Manager and the Lexical Handler. This interface is characterized by the Dialog Manager's need to receive inputs and to control the logical device properties described previously.

The first facet of the Lexical/Dialog Interface is the initialization of the logical devices. This includes passing of the lexical portions of the presentation description to the Lexical Handler. For example, a lexical handler may include a menu facility. Before any logical menu devices can be used a description of the menu is needed, including the order of the items, their text or icons, and possibly their command or control key equivalents. This information is stored as part of the lexical Presentation Description. The nature of lexical Presentation Descriptions and how they are created will be discussed later.

A logical device identifier must also be provided to the Lexical Handler. This logical device identifier is usually an integer number that the Lexical Handler will return to the Dialog Manager whenever that logical input has been entered by the user. The Dialog Manager will then use this logical device identifier in all future communication with the Lexical Handler.

The Lexical Handler must provide routines to the Dialog Manager for the following functions.

- Acquiring or Releasing a logical device or set of logical devices (such as a whole menu or a whole context).
- Enabling and Disabling of devices. The prompt and echo of a device should be visible whenever the device is enabled.
- A routine to get input events.
- Possibly, routines to sample inputs.

Lexical Implementations

Most current windowing systems and UIMSs want all inputs to be event inputs. This is particularly easy in the standard workstation configuration which has a mouse and a keyboard as the only input devices. The events such as mouse buttons, key presses, and function buttons can all be placed in an event record which is placed in a queue of events. The event record might appear as follows.

```
Event = Record
        EventCode:Integer;
        MouseX,MouseY:Integer;
        EventValue:Integer;
        Time: Integer;
End;
```

The EventCode contains a number identifying the physical input event that has occurred. Whenever any event occurs the mouse is sampled and its coordinates placed in MouseX and MouseY. In some cases there is a value associated with the event, such as a character code for the key struck or the presence of modifier keys such as shift or control. The Time field which indicates when the event occurred is optional and is generally ignored by the Dialog Manager, but may be used by some evaluation tools. Many systems provide more extensive information in the event record depending on the kind of event being returned.

Sampled Devices in Event Systems

Note that the mouse device is sampled every time another event occurs, even if the mouse location is not needed. This is not a serious overhead in today's workstations since it is usually a matter of reading a memory location. A problem arises, however, if one would like to continuously sample the mouse location when no other events are occurring. An example of this is when dragging an object. An event occurs when the mouse button is pressed over the object and an event occurs when the button is released. Between these events the mouse location is needed continuously so that the object can be moved.

In an event-only system the need for continuous input can be handled in one of two ways. The first is to create special NULL events. These events are returned whenever an event is requested from an empty event queue. NULL events will sample the mouse just as any other event would. In this fashion continuous inputs can be received from the sampled mouse device. If one does not want continuous mouse inputs the NULL event can be disabled.

Event-only Lexical Handlers are particularly attractive in multiprocessing systems such as X-Windows/UNIX. The device server process can take a physical event, check the mouse location against the window list, and forward the event to the process that owns that window. The NULL event approach, however, is unacceptable in a device server architecture because the server would flood the system with NULL events. An alternative scheme is to use mouse-movement events. Whenever the server sees that the mouse location has changed it will generate a

MouseMoved event, but only if MouseMoved is enabled. This approach will not only reduce the number of events generated but will also allow for multiple sampled devices. The simple NULL event approach described above would have a problem handling a bank of knobs as input devices because the model only returns mouse values. To return all possible sampled values would lead to excessive overhead and would be unnecessary since a user will rarely change more than one or two sampled inputs at a time. The Lexical Handler can then check all sampled input devices and generate events for any enabled devices that have changed.

A Lexical Handler that returns only events presents a very simple interface to the Dialog Handler. The event record becomes:

```
LogicalEvent = Record
        LogicalEventCode:Integer;
        DeviceValue: Measure;
    End;
```

In this case the DeviceValue is a union of all of the possible device measures that might be returned. Systems based on CORE and GKS have restricted measures to characters, scalar real numbers, points, and sequences of points. It may be desirable for Lexical Handlers to support other interactive techniques such as rubber-band lines or rubber-band rectangles. Some of the systems described later can support the addition of programmer-defined lexical techniques, in which case measures must be flexible enough to handle any application data.

In summary, the Lexical Handler must support logical device initialization with presentation information, acquiring and releasing of logical devices, enabling and disabling of logical devices, a routine to get events from the Lexical Handler's, event queue, and a routine to remove all events from the event queue.

Semantics

A key to many dialog models is their relationship with the application code. The generalized mapping to application code of UIMSs is the feature that allows their use in a wide variety of settings. There are two major models used for the Semantic Interface between the Dialog Manager and the Application Code. The command model views the application as a server which provides a set of command procedures that can be called by the user interface in order to get actions performed. The data model views the application as a data structure to be manipulated by the user interface. These two models are not mutually exclusive and, in fact, share components in many cases.

Command Model Semantics

There are several variations on the command model for the Semantic Interface. The simplest variation is a set of named commands to be called. These are usually the names of procedures in the Application Code. Each of the semantic procedures is expected to find its own arguments from the global information. For example, an EnterPoint action would call the Lexical Handler to get a copy of the current event record so that it could get the mouse coordinates.

Application access to the Lexical Handler is usually unacceptable because inappropriate calls may upset the working of the Dialog Manager. A simple extension is always to pass the current event record to each semantic procedure as a parameter. The overhead of this is reduced by only passing a pointer to the event record, and it eliminates application interference between the Dialog Manager and the Lexical Handler.

Both the simple command procedure and the fixed-event parameter procedures require only that the Dialog Descriptions store the name of the procedure. These models are rather inflexible in the kinds of information that can be propagated through the Dialog Description. A more sophisticated model allows each command procedure to have an arbitrary number of parameters. A problem arises as to the type of the parameters. A simple approach in languages like C is to allow any parameter that can be cast to a long integer. If the information is longer than a long integer then a pointer can be used. By using parameters of the same size, questions of argument type can be ignored. This also simplifies the implementation, as will be shown later. The most flexible model allows parameters of any user-defined type, and allows semantic procedures to return function results. In this model the UIMS can do type checking on the use of the semantic procedures in the Dialog Description. This model also requires that the Dialog Description be able to represent full semantic expressions instead of simple semantic procedure names. The Dialog Description must also have a model for passing data between various semantic expressions found in the dialog.

Data Model Semantics

A semantic data model is normally built around data objects or records that have several named attributes or fields associated with them. For example, a student object might have the following attributes:

- Name
- IDNumber
- Age

- Sex
- GPA

The attributes may be scalar values such as integers, reals, strings, or enumerated types, or they may be complex objects in their own right. The dialog operates on this semantic model by modifying the values of an object's attributes. Object-oriented programming systems are frequently used to implement this model. In addition, an object-oriented model might also supply methods on the object that allow the dialog to "do things" to the object rather than just modify its fields. This leads the data model towards the command model. Other semantic models in Lisp-based systems allow the attachment of guard expressions or demons to object attributes (or properties, as they are frequently called). These guards or demons are executed whenever the attributes are changed or, in some cases, when the attribute values are retrieved. A data model is the basis for the screen generator software frequently used in data processing applications.

A strict data model that does not allow for any code to be executed in response to data modifications would not form an acceptable semantic model, because there is insufficient power to model all of the user interface facilities that applications require. The difference between command and data models is not whether or not procedural code is executed but whether the dialog's primary view of the application is one of actions to be taken or of information to be manipulated.

Implementation of the Semantic Interface

There are a variety of ways to implement the Semantic Interface but only the most widely used are discussed here.

Simple Commands

The simple command model of semantics with procedure names only is the easiest to implement. Let us assume that our application has the following semantic commands.

        0 DeleteLine
        1 DrawLine
        2 DeleteCircle
        3 DrawCircle
        4 QuitProg

Let us also assume that the application programmer has written a procedure for each of the above commands and has given the procedure the prescribed name. In most command model interfaces we associate an integer number with each semantic command. This command number is used by the Dialog Manager when interfacing with the semantics. The simplest Semantic Interface is to generate a procedure that accepts the command number and then calls the correct procedure. The following is such a generated procedure in Pascal.

```
Procedure DoSemanticCommand( CommandNum:Integer );
  Begin
    Case CommandNum Of
      0: DeleteLine;
      1: DrawLine;
      2: DeleteCircle;
      3: DrawCircle;
      4: QuitProg;
    End;
  End; { DoSemanticCommand }
```

Some systems allow an arbitrary fragment of program text to be used as a semantic action. In such cases the program text fragment for a semantic action is generated where the procedure name was shown in the above example.

Some languages, such as C, allow the addresses of procedures to be stored in data structures. Using this facility of C one can generate the following code.

```
typedef (void *) SemanticCommand();
SemanticCommand  Semantics[] =
   {   DeleteLine,
       DrawLine,
       DeleteCircle,
       DrawCircle,
       QuitProg };

#define DoSemanticCommand(C) (*(Semantics[C]))()
```

Each of the two approaches described can be generated from a list of semantic commands derived from the Dialog Description. This code must be generated and then compiled with the Application Code. The Dialog Manager then simply calls DoSemanticCommand using whatever command numbers are stored in the Dialog Description.

In some cases it is desirable to define the Semantic Interface at run time to avoid the semantic interface generation and recompile step. A functional callback approach is possible in languages like C. This is the approach used in the X-Windows toolkit. The UIMS or windowing package maintains a symbol table for semantic functions (or callbacks as they are called in X-Windows). A simple interface might be:

```
void EnterCallBack( CmndName, CmndProc)
  char *CmndName;
  SemanticCommand CmndProc;
  {
  }
SemanticCommand LookUpCallBack( CmndName )
  char *CmndName;
  {
  }
```

This system requires the application code to register its semantic routines by means of the EnterCallBack procedure. The main program for our example would be:

```
  ...
  ...
EnterCallBack("DeleteLine",DeleteLine);
EnterCallBack("DrawLine",DrawLine);
EnterCallBack("DeleteCircle",DeleteCircle);
EnterCallBack("DrawCircle",DrawCircle);
EnterCallBack("QuitProg",QuitProg);
  ...
  ...
```

The UIMS would be called after the semantic commands have been registered. The Dialog Description would then store its semantic commands as string names. When the Dialog Description is read, the UIMS would look up the semantic names in the callback table and then build a table similar to the Semantics table defined in the generation approach. The invocation of semantic actions would then be the same as before.

A similar approach is possible in languages like Pascal which do not support storing the addresses of functions. In this case the Application Code must supply the DoSemantics procedure, which is written by hand. The application programmer, rather than the generator, would assign command numbers. The EnterCallBack routine would be passed a command number, rather than a function address, along with the command name.

The primary value of the callback table approach is that no generation step is required. This requires slightly more work on the part of the application programmer but in some cases may speed the interface modification process by eliminating the generate and recompile steps. This approach is used in windowing systems and toolkits whose intent is not to require any additional tools or generators beyond what can be handled by a subroutine package.

Single Parameter Commands

The Semantic Interface for models that use a fixed parameter is almost identical to that for simple command models. In this model the application programmer must write semantic commands that accept an EventRecord as a parameter. The generated procedure approach would output the following.

```
        Procedure DoSemanticCommand( CommandNum:Integer;
                Evnt: EventRecord );
        Begin
          Case CommandNum Of
            0: DeleteLine(Evnt);
            1: DrawLine(Evnt);
            2: DeleteCircle(Evnt);
            3: DrawCircle(Evnt);
            4: QuitProg(Evnt);
          End;
        End; { DoSemanticCommand }
```

The generated function address tables, of which the Semantics array was an example, would be the same because C does not care about how many parameters a procedure has. The invocation of the semantic commands would be changed to the following.

```
        #define DoSemanticCommand(C,E) (*(Semantics[C]))(E)
```

No changes other than in DoSemanticCommand are required when using the callback method for a Semantic Interface.

Multiparameter Commands

When we add multiple parameters to commands, only the generated case statement form of the Semantic Interface is possible. The Dialog Description must know the names of the semantic commands, the names and types of the parameters, and the result type. As an example the following semantic commands might be used.

```
0 DeleteLine( WhichLine: Line );
1 DrawLine( P1:Point; P2:Point );
2 DeleteCircle( WhichCircle: Circle );
3 DrawCircle( Center:Point; Radius:long );
4 PickCircle( SelectPoint: Point ):Circle;
5 PickLine( SelectPoint: Point ): Line;
6 QuitProg;
```

A simple model would be to assume that all parameters are long integers which can also store pointers. This assumption allows the parameter typing question to be ignored in the Dialog Description. However, the assumption does require that user-defined types like Point, Line, and Circle must either fit into a long integer or else a pointer to them must be used. The generated code for this fixed type model is then:

```
Const MaxCommandParms=6;
Type Parms = array [1..MaxCommandParms] of long;

Function DoCommand( CommandNum:Integer;
        P: Parms ):long;
  Begin
    DoCommand:=0;
    Case CommandNum Of
      0: DeleteLine(P[1]);
      1: DrawLine(P[1],P[2]);
      2: DeleteCircle(P[1]);
      3: DrawCircle(P[1],P[2]);
      4: DoCommand:=PickCircle( P[1] );
      5: DoCommand:=PickLine( P[1] );
      6: QuitProg;
    End;
  End; { DoCommand }
```

It is frequently undesirable to force UIMS users into a single word format for semantic values. It is also helpful in some cases if the Semantic Interface will also perform some type checking. If a semantic interface that supports full user types and type checking is desired then a type declaration must be generated which is a union of all the possible types and contains an indication of the particular value type. Such a system would generate the following.

```pascal
Type Value = Record
   Case ValueType:Integer of
      1: IntegerFld : Integer;
      2: RealFld : Real;
      3: StringFld : String;
      4: PointFld : Point;
      5: LineFld: Line;
      6: CircleFld: Circle;
   End;
Const MaxCommandParms=6;
Type Parms = array [1..MaxCommandParms] of Value;
Function DoCommand( CommandNum:Integer;P: Parms ):Value;
   Var Tmp:Value;
   Begin
      Tmp.ValueType:=0;
      Case CommandNum Of
         0:  If (P[1].ValueType=5) Then
             DeleteLine(P[1].LineFld);
         1:  If (P[1].ValueType=4) and(P[2].ValueType=4) Then
             DrawLine(P[1],P[2]);
         2:  If (P[1].ValueType=6) Then
             DeleteCircle(P[1].CircleFld);
         3:  If (P[1].ValueType=4) and(P[2].ValueType=1) Then
             DrawCircle(P[1],P[2]);
         4:  If (P[1].ValueType=4) Then
             Begin
                Tmp.ValueType:=6;
                Tmp.CircleFld:=PickCircle(
                   P[1].PointFld );
             End;
         5:  If (P[1].ValueType=4) Then
             Begin
                Tmp.ValueType=5;
                Tmp.LineFld:=PickLine(
                   P[1].PointFld);
             End;
         6:  QuitProg;
      End;
      DoCommand:=Tmp;
   End; { DoCommand }
```

Note that any primitive types that are known to the Lexical Handler (such

---

as Integer, Real, String, and Point) must always be present in the Value type and must always have the same numbers. This is so that the standard UIMS code can always put together a Value item for inputs received from the Lexical Handler.

Interpreted Semantic Actions

A final form of Semantic Interface is simply to use the facilities of an interpretive language. Lisp and its derivatives are very amenable to this form of semantic action. A command can be constructed as a Lisp list and then evaluated using Eval.

> (DrawLine '(12 134) '(12 160))

Several object-oriented languages allow for similar construction of messages at run time. The use of an interpretive language allows most command-based semantics to be derived directly from the Dialog Description without any additional effort.

Data Display

The on-screen images produced by a graphics application are one of the most important parts of the user interface and one of the least understood in UIMS research. Such graphical output includes the drawings being manipulated by a CAD (computer-aided design) package, the text being edited in a text editor, or the file icons in the Macintosh's Finder. These are the images that reflect the underlying data that are being manipulated by the application.

One of the goals of UIMS research has been to create descriptions for the data display that are similar to the dialog descriptions used by the Dialog Manager. The problem lies in handling the display of active data. As an interactive session progresses the underlying data in the application is modified in response to the semantic commands. As these modifications occur the application data display must be updated to reflect these changes.

Early UIMS research ignored the Data Display problem because this was considered a function of the application code. With the advent of direct manipulation interfaces this has changed. The essence of a direct manipulation interface is that the input is expressed in terms of manipulation of on-screen objects. A UIMS which does not directly relate input processing to the display of application data is only addressing half of the dialog. Although research is underway there are only a few results available that can be published here.

A key issue in developing automated support for Data Display is the problem of relating the visual images to the data they represent. Various schemes for this have been proposed both as part of object-oriented programming paradigms and in some UIMS research efforts. Each of these will be discussed in later chapters.

Dialog Manager

In almost all UIMS developments the Dialog Manager has been the heart of the research. The Dialog Manager is driven by the Dialog Description which contains a declarative representation of how the user interface is to function. This description must not only include the Semantic Interface and logical device specifications described above, but also define the mappings between the sequence of logical inputs received from the user and the semantic actions to be invoked.

The primary function of the Dialog Manager is to accept logical inputs from the Lexical Handler's event queue and decide what semantic actions to invoke and what information to pass to them. The Dialog Manager must inform the Lexical Handler as to when devices should be acquired and released as well as when they should be enabled and disabled. This is usually done by calling procedures supplied by the Lexical Handler.

The Dialog Manager is responsible for any help messages, error messages, or prompts that are to be given to the user. The Presentation Description will contain the actual content of such messages, but it is up to the Dialog Manager to decide when they are appropriate. It is also up to the Dialog Manager to handle any changes in visual context, such as moving from one set of windows to another when performing a different function. Such changes in visual context are closely related to the changes in input context that cause the acquiring and releasing of logical devices. When icons are used as part of logical input devices the relationship between input and visual context can become rather blurred, as we will see.

In later chapters we will discuss a number of advanced features that are also part of the Dialog Manager's responsibility. In the case of the Macros by Example research the Dialog Manager is responsible both for collecting the macro semantics and for interpreting the macros when they are invoked. In the discussion of measurement of user interface usage it is the Dialog Manager's responsibility to collect the raw information that the measurements and analysis are taken from.

Accessing the Semantic Interface is also a major function of the Dialog Manager. This is a relatively simple process in the case of parameterless or event-parameter commands. The command names must all be stored in the Dialog Description and then mapped to command numbers which are used throughout the rest of the description. In the case of semantic commands involving more than one parameter the dialog description must be able to store full expressions rather than simple command numbers. A particularly difficult problem is the storage of constants of user-defined data types. In the case of the primitive values known to the UIMS and the Lexical Handler, the space required and the storage format for each constant is known and can be provided for. In the case of user-defined data types the space required is variable and the format of the data in the application code may change after such a value is saved in the Dialog Description. Most UIMSs only store primitive values in their Dialog Descriptions and build up user-defined values at run time using semantic expressions. An exception to this is Lisp lists, which all have a standard form and thus do not suffer from the problems described.

When semantic commands with explicit parameters are used, the Dialog Model must support mechanisms for storing and propagating semantic values through the dialog. A simple example of this is as follows:

- the user selects the Line icon
- the user points at a location for one end-point which must be saved somewhere
- the user points at a second location which must be retrieved from the event and combined with the first end-point in a call on the DrawLine semantic command.

Each Dialog Model has its own mechanisms for propagating semantic values.

As has been discussed, the Dialog Description is the primary specification vehicle for the UIMS. As such it must be presented to dialog authors, graphics designers, dialog evaluators, and other user interface developers in a form suitable for human understanding. This external form of the Dialog Description is either textual or is edited by means of special interface design tools. The external Dialog Description frequently requires some analysis and/or recoding to be suitable for the Dialog Manager to use efficiently. To fill this need many UIMSs have user interface generators. These may either be a separate program or be built into the interface design tools.

The interface generator would also contain the generator for the Semantic Interface if one is required. The generator would also reduce the external Dialog Description into an internal Dialog Description. The internal Dialog Description usually consists of tables that drive the Dialog Manager and change textual command names to the internal command numbers. Some analysis might be performed on the dialog to determine when acquire/release and enable/disable operations should be performed. The semantic actions might be type checked. Some interface generators will also compute screen layouts from the semantic or dialog descriptions.

An Example

To understand this architecture let us look again at the simple drawing application.

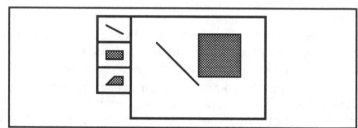

Figure 2:7
Simple Drawing Application

The functionality for this application might be described in a Semantic Interface such as:

```
DrawLine(X1,Y1,X2,Y2)
DrawRect(X1,Y1,X2,Y2)
StartPoly(X,Y)
AddPolyPoint(X,Y)
EndPoly()
```

The application code would implement these routines and would also manage a list of the draw objects to be displayed in the window. The three icons would be part of the Presentation Description and would be drawn on the screen by the Lexical Handler. Each icon might be associated with a logical input device such as LineInput, RectInput, and PolyInput. When the user clicks on a mouse button, the graphics package would send the physical MouseDown event to the Lexical Handler. The Lexical Handler would check the mouse location and find that the mouse is currently inside the rectangle icon. The Lexical Handler would then send the logical RectInput event on to the Dialog Manager. The Dialog Manager would remember that it is now trying to draw a rectangle. On two successive mouse clicks the Lexical Handler would see that the physical MouseDown events are inside of the draw area and would forward logical MouseDown events on to the Dialog Manager. The logical MouseDown event coordinates would have been converted into coordinates relative to the draw area by the Lexical Handler.

By looking at the Dialog Description the Dialog Manager would determine that the logical input sequence of RectInput, MouseDown, and MouseDown indicates that a rectangle should be drawn. The Dialog Manager would extract the mouse locations from the MouseDown events and pass them to the semantic routine DrawRect as parameters. In response to a call on DrawRect, the application code would add a new rectangle object to the list of objects in the draw area and would notify the Data Presentation of this fact. The Data Presentation, based on information in the Presentation Description, would update the draw area to display the new rectangle. This updating is done by calls on the Graphics Package.

Summary

The architecture of most UIMSs contains several of the components described in this chapter although some, or most, of the components will be omitted in some cases. The Lexical Handler provides the basic input capability. The lexical interface described above will suffice for most UIMS models. The Semantic Interface provides the mechanism for generalizing the UIMS across a variety of applications and for tying the dialog model to the application. Semantic models have been described in detail here since they are found throughout all UIMSs. The only major semantic model not discussed is the object-oriented model. This will be covered in detail later as it is intimately tied to the object-oriented and data dialog models. The data display component must provide the mapping between application data and the visual images that represent it. Models for this component are still in their infancy. The Dialog Manager is the heart of most UIMSs and it is the implementation of the Dialog Model that drives each UIMS. Dialog Models and their impact on UIMS implementation will be the topic of most of the chapters in this book.

References

1 Foley, J.D. and V.L. Wallace. *The Art of Natural Graphic Man-Machine Conversation.* **Proceedings of the IEEE** 62(4): 462-70, April 1974.

2 *Status Report of the Graphic Standards Planning Committee.* **Computer Graphics** 13(3), August 1979.

3 *Graphical Kernel System.* **Computer Graphics**, Special GKS Issue, February 1984.

4 Wallace, V.L. *The Semantics of Graphic Input Devices.* Proceedings of SIGGRAPH/SIGPLAN Conference on Graphics Languages. **Computer Graphics** 10(1): 61-65, April 1976.

5 Rosenthal, D.S.H., J.C. Michener, G.E. Pfaff, R. Kessener, and M. Sabin. *The Detailed Semantics of Graphics Input Devices.* **Computer Graphics** 16(3): 33-38, July 1982.

3.
State Machine UIMSs

The state machine has been the basis for more UIMSs than any other dialog form, perhaps because of its natural form for specifying what should happen next. The earliest state machine system was Newman's Reaction Handler.[1] Several state machine systems have been reported by Wasserman,[2] Feldman and Rogers,[3] Jacobs,[4] Edmonds,[5] and Olsen,[6] to name a few.

This chapter will not explore all the various state machine systems but will concentrate on the major architectural features of state machines. The basic algorithms are not complicated and can be easily implemented. The simple state machine is presented first, along with its interfaces to the lexical and semantic portions of a UIMS. The notion of a recursive state machine allows the dialog to be structured into subdialogs with the accompanying notion of contexts. Pervasive states allow global facilities to be specified simply and in one place. Mechanisms that allow the application semantics to control the interactive dialog are then introduced. Finally, an overall evaluation of the state machine approach to UIMSs is given.

Simple State Machines

An example of a simple state machine is shown below.

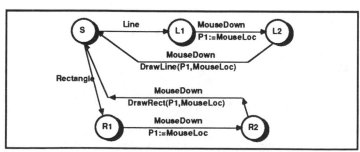

Fig. 3:1
Simple State Machine

The dialog starts out in state S. When it receives either the logical input Line or Rectangle it proceeds to state L1 or R1, respectively. In state L1, if the logical input MouseDown is received, the semantic action "P1:=MouseLoc" is executed and the machine proceeds to state L2. Following a dialog state by state though the above diagram is an easy concept to grasp. Such diagrams form an external dialog description which can be translated into internal tables.

Although state diagrams like that shown above appear frequently in UIMS papers, many UIMS implementations do not use them. They are often not used because, 1) they require an interactive graphical editor for creation, 2) extended semantic expressions are difficult to specify in a diagram, 3) the diagrams consume a large amount of screen space, and 4) a significant amount of effort is required to keep a large diagram orderly and readable. These problems hamper efforts to use such dialog descriptions for large problems.

Many state machine UIMSs use a textual language for specifying the dialog. A textual version of the state diagram is given below.

```
State Start:
  On Line Then L1;
  On Rectangle Then R1;
State L1:
  On MouseDown
    Do P1:=MouseLoc;
    Then L2;
State L2:
  On MouseDown
    Do DrawLine(P1,MouseLoc);
    Then Start;
State R1:
  On MouseDown
    Do P1:=MouseLoc;
    Then R2;
State R2:
  On MouseDown
    Do DrawRect(P1,MouseLoc);
    Then Start;
```

This example is not taken from any particular system but gives a general feel for such textual specifications.

Neither the state diagram nor the textual language is suitable for use at run time by the dialog manager. Each of these external descriptions must be translated into an internal description. Such internal descriptions consist primarily of a table of transitions of the form.

(CurrentState, Input, Action, NextState)

Using this form the state machine described above becomes:

(Start,Line,,L1)
(Start,Rectangle,,R1)
(L1,MouseDown,P1:=MouseLoc,L2)
(L2,MouseDown,DrawLine(...),Start)
(R1,MouseDown,P1:=MouseLoc,R2)
(R2,MouseDown,DrawRect(...),Start)

The transitions above are shown with state names for clarity. In an actual implementation the state names are converted to integers. The dialog manager then follows the simple algorithm:

```
CurrentState:=Start;
Repeat
  {
  GetEvent(E);
  Select a transition T using CurrentState and E
  DoCommand(Action(T));
  CurrentState:=NextState(T);
  }
```

The key to this algorithm is the selection of a transition based on the current state and the logical event received. If the transitions are stored in a list like that shown above, the selection process simply looks at each transition in turn matching the current state and the event. In the case of a large number of transitions this matching process can be very slow. Compilers and hardware that use state machines use a table like that shown below.

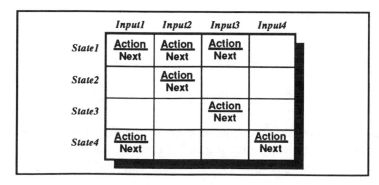

	Input1	*Input2*	*Input3*	*Input4*
State1	**Action** **Next**	**Action** **Next**	**Action** **Next**	
State2		**Action** **Next**		
State3			**Action** **Next**	
State4	**Action** **Next**			**Action** **Next**

Fig. 3:2
State Table

Such state tables are fast and easily implemented, but they are rather sparse and consume a lot of memory. The following transition list per state form is a good compromise between the need for speed and the need to conserve memory.

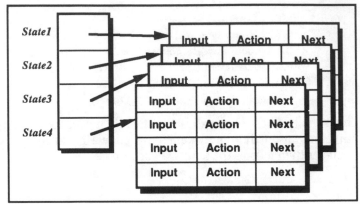

Fig. 3:3
Transition List

The dialog manager need only keep up with people time which, in terms of computer cycles, is very long, but the dialog management algorithm cannot be excessively slow or operations such as dragging, which must handle events in less than one-fifth of a second, will exhibit poor performance.

Enable/Disable

The simple dialog handler algorithm is easily augmented to handle the enabling and disabling of logical devices. This algorithm is shown below.

```
CurrentState:=Start;
Repeat
  { Disable all devices;
  Enable all devices on transitions
    leaving CurrentState;
  GetEvent(E);
  Select a transition T using CurrentState and E
  DoCommand(Action(T));
  CurrentState:=NextState(T);
  }
```

This approach enables only those devices on transitions leaving the current state, since such devices are the only acceptable inputs. In the case of state S, in our example state machine, the enabled logical devices would be Line and Rectangle. The simple approach of disabling all devices and then enabling only those that leave the current state is frequently optimized by disabling only devices that were enabled in the previous state but should not be enabled in the current state.

Recursive State Machines

When faced with a user interface with hundreds of states the simple state machine becomes unmanageable. The model is extended by adding subdialogs which are logically equivalent to procedures in a conventional programming language. One can think of subdialogs as nonterminals in formal language and compiler theory. The following is an example of a state machine with a subdialog.

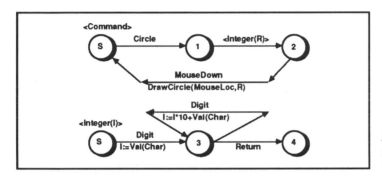

Fig. 3:4

State Machine with Subdialog

In the example above the main dialog has a command that will draw a circle, which first requires that the radius be typed as an integer. Since the typing of an integer may be required in several parts of the dialog we create a subdialog called <Integer>. This subdialog has its own start state.

One problem that arises is when to enter the subdialog and when to leave it. In the example shown above the subdialog <Integer> appears between states 1 and 2. In the subdialog the statement Return appears between states 3 and 4. We understand, conceptually, what we want to happen when a subdialog is invoked or terminated, but the question is, "how should this be handled in the algorithm?" One solution is to have the actual calling and returning handled by special semantic functions which can occur in the action expression of a transition. These semantic functions are defined below, along with the modified dialog-handling algorithm that will use them.

```
Call( SubDialog)
  { CallState = StartState(SubDialog); }
Return( )
  { ReturnFlag = True; }
```

Dialog Handler Algorithm

```
CS=StartState(MainDialog);
StateStack=empty;
CallState=0;
ReturnFlag=False;
Repeat
  (If not (CallState == 0) Then
    { Push CS onto StateStack;
    CS=CallState;
    CallState=0;
    }
  Else If (ReturnFlag) Then
    { CS = Pop(StateStack);
    ReturnFlag=False;
    }
  Disable all devices;
  Enable all devices on transitions
    leaving CS;
  GetEvent(E);
  Select a transition T using CS and E
  DoCommand(Action(T));
  CS=NextState(T);
  }
```

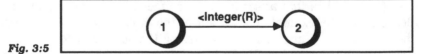

Fig. 3:5

The call and return actions can now be incorporated into the action expressions of transitions, but the issue of when those transitions should be taken is still not resolved. In the case of the transition we want the subdialog to be entered immediately because there are no other choices leaving state 1. We can handle this with a special input selector called NOW. The NOW selector indicates that one should not wait for any inputs but should take the specified transition immediately. In the case of the return from the <Integer> subdialog we can leave whenever a MouseDown event occurs. The new state machine is shown below in textual form.

```
<Command>
  State S:
    On Circle Then 1;
  State 1:
    NOW Do {Call(<Integer(R)>); } Then 2;
  State 2:
    On MouseDown Do
      { DrawCircle(MouseLoc,R); }
      Then S;
<Integer(I)>
  State S:
    On Digit Do
      {I=Val(Char);} Then 3;
  State 3:
    On Digit Do
      { I=I*10+Val(Char); } Then 3;
    On MouseDown Do
      { Return( ); } Then 4;
```

MouseDown was a good choice to return on because it is the next input that the user should enter, and we know that a MouseDown cannot be part of an integer. The problem is that the MouseDown that occurs between states 3 and 4 has already been used. State 2, after the return, now requires an additional MouseDown event which is not what we wanted at all. We can remedy this problem with an additional semantic function HoldInput(). The purpose of this function is to inhibit getting a new input so that the current input can be used again by a later transition. HoldInput is defined below along with the modified dialog handling algorithm that can process HoldInput and NOW.

```
HoldInput( )
  { HoldFlag=True; }
```

Dialog Handler Algorithm

```
CurrentState=StartState(MainDialog);
StateStack=empty;
CallState=0;
ReturnFlag=False;
HoldFlag=False;
Repeat
  {If not (CallState == 0) Then
     { Push CurrentState onto StateStack;
     CurrentState=CallState;
     CallState=0;
     }
  Else If (ReturnFlag) Then
     { CurrentState = Pop(StateStack);
     ReturnFlag=False;
     }
  Disable all devices;
  if (not HoldFlag)
     { Evnt=NULL;
     For each transition T
           leaving CurrentState
        { If (Input(T) == NOW ) Then
           {Evnt=NOW;}
        Else { Enable(Input(T)); }
     If (Evnt!=NOW) Then
        GetEvent(Evnt);
     }
  Select a transition T using CurrentState and Evnt
  DoCommand(Action(T));
  CurrentState=NextState(T);
  }
```

The HoldInput semantic action can also be used when calling subdialogs such as the following modification of the Circle command.

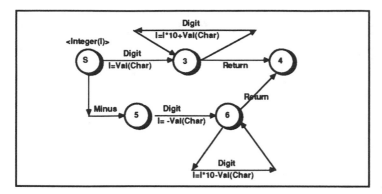

Fig. 3:7

In this example a NOW transition is not acceptable for calling <Integer> because a MouseDown event would indicate that <Integer> should not be called. With HoldInput the specification would be:

```
<Command>
  State S:
    On Circle Then 1;
  State 1:
    On Digit Do
      {HoldInput();
      Call(<Integer(R)>); } Then 2;
    On MouseDown Do
      { P1=MouseLoc; } Then 3;
  State 2:
    On MouseDown Do
      { DrawCircle(MouseLoc,R); }
      Then S;
  State 3:
    On MouseDown Do
      {DrawCircle(MouseLoc,
          Distance(MouseLoc,P1)); }
      Then S;
```

What we did was to look at the subdialog <Integer> and notice that it always started with Digit. We then made the call to <Integer> conditional upon the Digit event. This works well as long as the subdialog <Integer> starts only with a Digit. Suppose, however, the <Integer> dialog were changed to handle negative numbers, as follows.

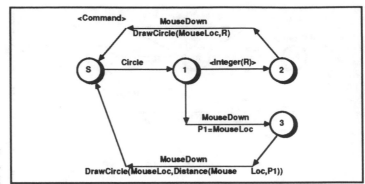

Fig. 3:6
Modified Circle Command

The <Integer> subdialog can now start with either a Digit or a Minus. If the invocation of <Integer> at state 1 is not changed to accept a Minus, a negative number can never be entered because without a Digit, <Integer> will never be invoked. A solution to this is to automatically propagate the starting events of a subdialog up to all of the subdialog's invocations. For example, the following external description.

```
<Command>
  State S:
    On Circle Then 1;
  State 1:
    On <Integer(R)> Then 2;
    On MouseDown Do
      { P1=MouseLoc; } Then 3;
  State 2:
    On MouseDown Do
      { DrawCircle(MouseLoc,R); }
      Then S;
  State 3:
    On MouseDown Do
      {DrawCircle(MouseLoc,
          Distance(MouseLoc,P1)); }
      Then S;
```

would be translated automatically into

```
(S, Circle,, 1)
(1, Digit,{ HoldInput(); Call(<Integer(R)>);},2 )
(1, Minus,{ HoldInput(); Call(<Integer(R)>);},2 )
(1, MouseDown,{ P1=MouseLoc; }, 3)
(2, MouseDown, { DrawCircle(MouseLoc,R); }, S)
(3, MouseDown, {DrawCircle(MouseLoc,
    Distance(MouseLoc,P1)); }, S)
```

The translation algorithm finds all uses of a subdialog as an input, replaces them with transitions that use the starting events of that subdialog, and puts HoldInput and Call in the action expressions. Several transformations of the external specification have been developed.[6] Most of the other transformations, because of their complexity, were more confusing than helpful to dialog authors.

Contexts on Subdialogs

Acquiring and releasing of logical devices, as well as handling of screen layouts, are associated with contexts. A context consists of a screen or window layout and a set of acquired devices. In order to delimit when a user is in a particular context we associate the context with a subdialog. When a user enters the subdialog the context associated with it is entered. When the user leaves the subdialog the context that existed before entry is returned to. Subdialogs are also used for structuring the interactive dialog and so not all of them have an associated context.

A key issue is how contexts are determined. A simple approach is to have the dialog author attach a list of acquired devices to each subdialog that is a new context. This solution requires that the dialog author constructs this list carefully, without missing any logical devices that might be needed within the subdialog and without including any unnecessary devices.

An alternative approach is to automatically compute the acquired device lists for those subdialogs that are new contexts. Computation of this list can be stated as follows.

DevicesUsed(SD) = the set of logical input devices that appear
 in any of the transitions of the subdialog SD.
SimpleSDsCalled(SD) = the set of subdialogs that are not
 defined as contexts and are invoked by some
 transition of SD.
AcquiredDevices(SD) = DevicesUsed(SD) +
 for all CD in SimpleSDsCalled(SD)
  add the AcquiredDevices(CD)

Note that the acquired devices of a given subdialog include not only the devices that it uses but also all of the devices that are used by the noncontext subdialogs that it calls, since those subdialogs do not create new contexts of their own.

The algorithm for handling contexts is as follows.

```
CurrentState=StartState(MainDialog);
CurrentContext = Context(MainDialog)
Acquire all devices in CurrentContext
StateStack=empty; ContextStack = Empty;
CallState=0;
ReturnFlag=False; HoldFlag=False;
Repeat
  {If not (CallState == 0) Then
    { Push CurrentState onto StateStack;
    if (CallState has a context) then
      { Release all devices in CurrentContext
      Push CurrentContext onto ContextStack;
      CurrentContext = Context(CallState);
      Acquire all devices in CurrentContext;
      }
    else
      {push NULL onto ContextStack }
      CurrentState=CallState;
      CallState=0;
      }
  Else If (ReturnFlag) Then
    { if (top(ContextStack) == NULL)
    { pop ContextStack ; }
    else
      { Release all devices in CurrentContext;
      CurrentContext = Pop(ContextStack);
      Acquire all devices in CurrentContext;
      }
    CurrentState = Pop(StateStack);
    ReturnFlag=False;
    }
  . . . . . . . .
  }
```

Semantic Attributes

All of the semantic actions used so far must communicate with each other via global variables inside the application code. Semantic communication inside the application code tends to obscure the relationships between the semantic actions, and is frequently awkward for dialog designers who prefer not to understand the inner workings of the application code. An alternative technique is derived from the attribute grammars found in compiler construction.[7] Every subdialog is given a set of zero or more semantic attributes. The types of these attributes depend on the form of the semantic interface described in chapter 2. For this discussion we will assume that there exists a type, Value, which can be used for all attribute values, and that the semantic interface will sort out any of the value typing and storage issues.

Local, Synthesized, and Inherited Attributes

For a given nonterminal we can define three kinds of attributes: synthesized, inherited, and local. Synthesized attributes are values that the subdialog returns to its invocation. Inherited attributes are values that the subdialog receives from its invocation. Local attributes are storage places used within the subdialog that are not part of the subdialog's invocation interface. These three kinds of attributes can be viewed as output parameters, input parameters, and local variables to a procedure (the subdialog). The following is an example of how attributes would be used.

```
<Command(LineWidth)>
  State S:
    On Circle Then 1;
  State 1:
    On Digit Do
      {HoldInput();
      Call(<Integer(R)>); } Then 2;
    On MouseDown Do
      { P1=MouseLoc; } Then 3;
  State 2:
    On MouseDown Do
      {DrawCircle(MouseLoc,R,LineWidth); }
      Then S;
  State 3:
    On MouseDown Do
      {DrawCircle(MouseLoc,
          Distance(MouseLoc,
            P1),LineWidth); }
      Then S;
```

In this example LineWidth is an inherited attribute from wherever the <Command> subdialog is called. R and P1 are local attributes of <Command>. The subdialog <Integer> has a single synthesized attribute which passes back the integer that was entered.

Extending the Algorithm

Extending the algorithm consists primarily of allocating space for the attributes and making sure that the inherited attributes are passed in correctly and that the synthesized attributes are passed out. A number of strategies from compiler construction could be used. Since the time demands for subdialog invocation are not critical, one of the simpler strategies is justified.

A stack of attributes is used with each subdialog referencing its own attributes relative to the top of the stack. The following diagram shows how the top of the stack is laid out.

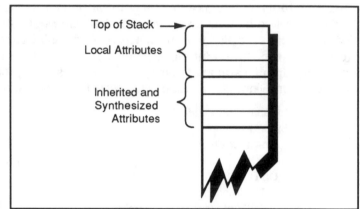

Fig. 3:8

When a subdialog is called, all arguments for inherited attributes are copied onto the stack and NULL values are used for synthesized or local attributes. When a subdialog returns, the local and inherited attributes are discarded and the synthesized attribute values are copied into their appropriate arguments. In the argument expressions for subdialog calls and for semantic actions, each attribute used in the argument expression is identified by its offset relative to the top of the stack.

The following is the modified dialog handling algorithm.

```
Call( SubDialog, Args)
  { CallState = StartState(SubDialog);
  for each argument A in Args from left to right do
    { If A corresponds to an inherited attribute
      {push value of A onto
       AttributeStack
     else /* is synthesized */
       { push NULL value
         onto AttributeStack }
      }
  for each local attribute of SubDialog
      push NULL value onto AttributeStack;
  Push (SubDialog,Args) onto CallStack;
   }
Return( )
  { ReturnFlag = True;
  pop (SubDialog,Args) from CallStack;
  for each local attribute of the current SubDialog
    pop AttributeStack
  for each argument A of Args from right to left do
    { If A corresponds to an inherited attribute
      { pop AttributeStack }
     else /* is synthesized */
       {pop AttributeStack and assign to A }
      }
 }
```

Dialog Handler Algorithm

```
CS=StartState(MainDialog);
StateStack=empty;
AttributeStack = empty;
CallStack = empty;
CallState=0;
ReturnFlag=False;
Repeat
  { . . . . .
   }
```

When Call is invoked it is passed a list of arguments. These arguments are attributes of the dialog that is invoking the new subdialog. As such, the

Args list is simply a list of stack offsets which indicate where to get inherited values from and where to put the returned synthesized attributes. If the argument was an expression then the dialog preprocessor should create local attributes that can store the result of the expression.

Pervasive States

The state machine model for dialogs proliferates states and transitions when some kinds of dialog features are added. Take, for example, the following state machine.

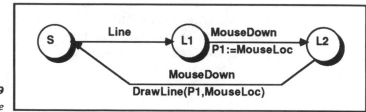

Fig. 3:9
State Machine

A nice feature to add to this dialog would be the ability to enter a HOME input to return the user to the start state. This feature could be provided in the following way.

Adding additional transitions to every state can get messy if the dialog has a large number of states. If other features, such as help or a calculator, are also necessary then every state becomes a rat's nest of crossing transition lines.

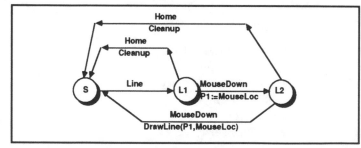

Fig. 3:10
HOME Feature

An alternative strategy is provided by pervasive states. A pervasive state is one which is always available regardless of the current state. Two kinds of pervasive states have been studied. They are escape states, which permanently change the dialog flow, and reenter states, which handle temporary deviations which then return to the original status of the machine.

Escape

Escape states are states whose transitions permanently leave the original flow of control. Such a state is pervasive in the sense that one is in the escape state simultaneously with all of the other states. Take the following case which solves the HOME problem described earlier.

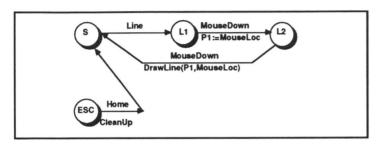

Fig. 3:11
HOME Feature

The special ESC state is always present. If, for example, the dialog was in the L2 state and HOME was entered, the transition from ESC would be taken because there is no transition from L2 on HOME. The algorithm is modified in the following way.

```
CS:=Start;
Repeat
  { Disable all devices;
  Enable all devices on transitions
    leaving CS;
  Enable all devices on transitions
    leaving ESC;
  GetEvent(E);
  if Select a transition T using CS and E
  else Select a transition T using ESC and E
  DoCommand(Action(T));
  CS:=Next(T);
  }
```

Note that in this algorithm the transitions leaving ESC have lower priority than those leaving the current state. If both the current state and ESC had transitions on some input, I, the transition from the current state would always override the transition leaving ESC. In the presence of subdialogs the escape states are treated like the start states. Every subdialog has its own escape state as well as its own start state.

Reenter

The purpose of a reenter state is to permit temporary deviations from the normal dialog flow and then to return to what was being done before. As in the case of escape states, each subdialog would have a reenter state whose transitions are pervasive. The following is an example of such a machine.

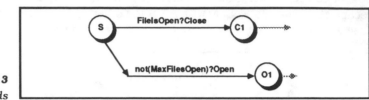

Fig. 3:13
Guards

In the above machine the user might be in state L2 and need to do some calculations. By entering the Calculate input the transition from RE would be taken and the <Calculator> subdialog would be invoked. Upon returning from <Calculator> the NOW transition from R1 would be taken, immediately causing a Return to be performed. The return would, however, not leave this subdialog but would rather return to state L2 which is where the reenter began from. This use of transitions from the reenter state allows the calculator to be invoked from any point in the dialog without interfering with whatever was currently underway.

The revised algorithm for handling pervasive inputs is:

```
CS:=Start;
Repeat
  { Disable all devices;
  Enable all devices on transitions
    leaving CS;
  Enable all devices on transitions
    leaving ESC;
  Enable all devices on transitions
    leaving RE;
  GetEvent(E);
  if Select a transition T using CS and E
  else if Select a transition T using RE and E
    { push CS onto the call stack;
    CS := RE
    }
  else Select a transition T using ESC and E
  DoCommand(Action(T));
  CS:=Next(T);
  }
```

Examination of the algorithm shows that transitions leaving a reenter state have lower priority than those leaving the current state and have higher priority than those leaving the escape state. This choice of priorities is simply an heuristic that was found to be effective in the IPDA (Interactive PushDown Automata)[6] research.

Semantic Control

So far in this chapter, the decisions controlling the course of the dialog have all been based on the current state and the current input event. In some cases the application semantics need to control how the dialog should proceed and what should be done next. For example, a command to close a file should not be interactively available if there is no file open. If a user has not entered a correct account and password, then the dialog should remain in the login sequence. Each of these represent conditions that must control the dialog but are not amenable to representation in a state machine model. The state machine cannot, or should not, represent all the possible combinations of open and closed files. Similarly, the state machine must consult the user database to locate acceptable user ID/password combinations.

Two forms are possible for semantic control of a dialog. The first is the notion of guards which can inhibit unacceptable inputs. The second is the idea of conditional transitions which can branch to various parts of a dialog based on some condition. The primary difference between these two forms is in the ease of expressing various semantic control solutions.

Guards

A guard, or guarded transition, places a Boolean semantic expression on a transition. If the guard expression is false, then the corresponding transition is not available for use by the next input. This guard can be any semantic expression that returns a Boolean result and is thus free to handle semantic conditions that require such control. The following is an example state machine that uses guarded transitions to determine which commands to allow.

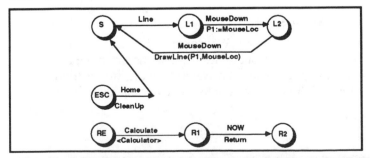

Fig. 3:12
Reenter

If the expression FileIsOpen returns false then the transition from S to C1 is temporarily not present and the logical input Close is disabled. If Close is a menu item then it might by grayed out, for example. If the expression MaxFilesOpen returns true then the transition from S to O1 would not be available and Open is disabled. The algorithm to handle guards is as follows.

Dialog Handler Algorithm

```
CS=StartState;
Repeat
  {  Disable all devices;
  E=NULL;
  For each transition T leaving CS
    { If Guard(T) Then
      {If (Input(T) == NOW ) Then
         {E=NOW;}
      Else {
         Enable(Input(T));
         }
      }
    }
  If not( E==NOW ) Then
    GetEvent(E);
  Select a transition T using CS and E
    where Guard(T) is true
  DoCommand(Action(T));
  CS=NextState(T);
  }
```

Note that a guard expression could be evaluated twice. Once when the devices are enabled and once when the transitions are being selected. Since the guard expression can be any Boolean expression, this double evaluation is potentially very costly. A better approach is to mark each transition's viability at the time that the devices are enabled and then check the marks only when selecting transitions.

Conditional Transitions

Conditional transitions take a more active approach to controlling a dialog than the guarded transitions. Conditional transitions are more applicable to situations where an overall control decision is made, rather than simple masking of a transition. Take, for example, the following login dialog.

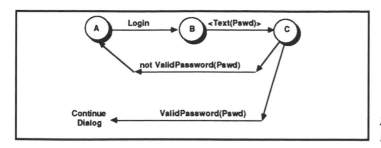

Fig. 3:14
Login Dialog

When the user reaches state C the password will have been entered and stored in the local attribute Pswd. If this is a valid password then the transition to continue the dialog should be taken. A conditional transition has a Boolean semantic expression as its input selector. If this expression is true then the input is converted to a NOW selector which will cause that transition to be immediately taken. This behavior is easily implemented as a guard on a transition with a NOW selector.

Summary of State Machine Approaches

The state machine model for dialog control is a straightforward approach. The concept of states from which branches are taken is easy to teach and relatively easy to implement. State diagrams are easy for most computer-literate people to learn. The problem that arises is one of scale. When there are 150 commands, each with three or four states, the diagram form becomes totally unmanageable. The textual form is basically a large GOTO-based program. The GOTO paradigm is one that has been generally rejected as an acceptable control model in most software engineering work. Some help comes from the structuring of the interface around subdialogs, which makes the understanding of a particular piece much easier. Complex branching is not a problem if the dialog fragment is small.

Unfortunately, the state machine model leads to interface designs where the user can do only one thing at a time. This complaint is partly a design problem. If one designs a dialog consisting of short, two or three-state sequences, which then lead back to the home state, the user's commitment to a particular activity is short enough not to matter. The use of pervasive states also helps to alleviate the sequential restrictions of state machines. There is still the problem, however, of trying to capture all of what it is acceptable to do next within the notion of a single, state. Frequently, the interface has many independent or semi-independent pieces of state information. Later chapters will discuss models for dealing with such issues.

In terms of the personnel roles in interface design, the state machine model caters only to the dialog author. The concept of moving from state to state upon given inputs is not difficult to teach to nonprogrammers, but the complexity of large state machines and the resulting decomposition into a hierarchy of subdialogs can become a problem for nonprogrammers. The issue of which inputs will invoke which subdialogs is particularly confusing.

In terms of the architecture the state machine lies squarely in the dialog handler. The description of the state machine would lie in the dialog description. The interface to the application semantics is handled by any of the suggested schemes, with the calls to semantic routines being placed on the transitions. In terms of the lexical interface, state machines offer one of the simplest approaches. Enable and disable issues are resolved by looking at the transitions leaving a state. Acquire and release issues are resolved by associating contexts with some of the subdialogs. Algorithms have also been shown for computing the context device sets automatically.

References

1 Newman, W. *A System for Interactive Graphical Programming.* **SJCC.** Washington, DC: Thompson Books, 1968, 47-54.

2 Wasserman, A.I. *User Software Engineering and the Design of Interactive Systems.* **Proceedings of the Fifth International Conference on Software Engineering,** March 1981.

3 Feldman, M. and G. Rogers. *Toward the Design and Development of Style-Independent Interactive Systems.* **Proceedings of Human Factors in Computer Systems** March, 1982, 111-16.

4 Jacob, R. *Using Formal Specifications in the Design of a Human-Computer Interface.* **Proceedings of Human Factors in Computer Systems,** March, 1982 315-22.

5 Edmonds, E.A. *The Man-Computer Interface—a Note on Concepts and Design.* **International Journal of Man Machine Studies** 16, 1982.

6 Olsen, D. *Push-down Automata for User Interface Management.* **ACM Transactions on Graphics** 3(3): 177-203, July 1984.

7 Aho, A.V., R. Sethi, and J.D. Ullman. **Compilers: Principles, Techniques and Tools.** New York: Addison-Wesley, 1986, 279-342.

4.
Grammar UIMSs

Using a grammar to describe a user interface is natural, since parsing of user inputs is essentially language processing. Menu items and function buttons replace the traditional keywords and delimiters. The problem is to take a sequence of input events, determine if it is correct, and invoke the appropriate semantic actions.

An early use of grammars in the context of a UIMS was reported by Hanau and Lenorovitz.[1] They applied the existing YACC parser generator found on most UNIX systems to a different set of lexical inputs. Instead of using LEX, as is usual, they supplied a graphical lexical handler to provide the inputs. This approach was only used as a prototyping tool and was not incorporated into a production UIMS.

A more complete grammar-based UIMS was the SYNGRAPH system.[2] SYNGRAPH accepted a set of logical device definitions and a grammar that defined the dialog. From this description a file of Pascal code was generated and compiled with the application code to form a complete interactive application.

This chapter describes the basic algorithms used with a grammar UIMS, and discusses several user interface features that were developed specially for grammars but were not applicable for a nongrammar-based UIMS.

Basic Parse Algorithm

The following is an example grammar which describes an interactive dialog.

```
<Dialog> ::= <Command>
<Command> ::=
  LINE MouseDown [P1:=MouseLoc]
    MouseDown [DrawLine(P1,MouseLoc)]
```

```
<Command>
| RECTANGLE MouseDown [P1=MouseLoc]
  MouseDown [DrawRect(P1,MouseLoc) ]
  <Command>
| ....
| ....
| QUIT
```

In this grammar, nonterminals (enclosed in angle brackets) serve the same function as subdialogs in the state machine model. The terminals appear in the order in which they should occur. Terminals in the dialog description map directly to logical input devices. In the above example QUIT, LINE, MouseDown, and RECTANGLE are logical devices. Semantic actions are enclosed in square brackets. The vertical bar stands for alternation. A <Command> consists of LINE followed by MouseDown and MouseDown, or RECTANGLE followed by MouseDown and MouseDown. The grammar notation eliminates the need to specify a lot of states. The natural sequence of each production controls the sequencing rather than specifying a state between each input. This natural sequentiality can cause problems, however, when attempting to provide options or repeated items. Such things can still be done but require more thought in constructing the dialog grammar. Extensions to simple grammars, which eliminate some of these problems, will be discussed later.

Note, that in ordinary grammars iteration is accomplished by means of recursion, as in the case of <Command> at the end of LINE and RECTANGLE. The algorithms we will discuss can handle this form of recursion without producing a buildup on the stack that most recursion causes.

The basic dialog handling algorithm then proceeds as follows.

```
Push Start nonterminal on a stack
While Stack not empty do
  { S := Pop top symbol from stack;
  If (S is a terminal) then
    {GetEvent(E);
    If not (E == S) then
      { report an error;
      push S back onto the stack;
      }
    }
  Else If (S is an action) then
    {DoCommand(S); }
```

```
    Else If (S has only one production P) then
       { Push symbols of P on the stack in reverse order }
    Else
       {GetEvent(E)
       Select a production P using E
       If (no production is selected) Then
            { report an error;
            Push S back onto the stack
            }
          else
            {Push all symbols in P, except the first one,
                onto the stack in reverse order.
            }
       }
    }
```

The key to the algorithm is selecting a production based on the current event. In traditional LL(1) parser construction, formal definitions are given for computing the select set for each production. However, it has been found that the complex select sets required in compilers are too confusing for dialog authors to use. Such computations are not really required when generating interactive dialogs for which simple syntax is a virtue. We can guarantee simple select sets if we require that all productions start with a logical input device. Then the algorithm need only compare the first symbol of each production of a nonterminal with the current event in order to select the correct production.

The following sequence of steps shows how the dialog handler algorithm works. The sequence of inputs is given with the current event highlighted in bold face. The stack is shown with the top item on the stack highlighted.

Input: **LINE** MouseDown(10,20) MouseDown(20,30) QUIT
Stack: **<Dialog>**
   select the only production for Dialog
====================================
Input: **LINE** MouseDown(10,20) MouseDown(20,30) QUIT
Stack: **<Command>**
   Enable LINE, RECTANGLE, QUIT
====================================

Input: LINE **MouseDown(10,20)** MouseDown(20,30) QUIT
Stack: <Command> [DrawLine ...] MouseDown [P1=...] **MouseDown**
  Select the first production of <Command>
  Enable MouseDown

======================================

Input: LINE MouseDown(10,20) **MouseDown(20,30)** QUIT
Stack: <Command> [DrawLine ...] MouseDown **[P1=...]**
  Do action [P1:=(10,20)]

======================================

Input: LINE MouseDown(10,20) **MouseDown(20,30)** QUIT
Stack: <Command> [DrawLine ...] **MouseDown**
  Enable: MouseDown

======================================

Input: LINE MouseDown(10,20) MouseDown(20,30) **QUIT**
Stack: <Command> **[DrawLine ...]**
  Do action [DrawLine((10,20), (20,30))]

======================================

Input: LINE MouseDown(10,20) MouseDown(20,30) **QUIT**
Stack: **<Command>**
  Enable LINE, RECTANGLE, QUIT

======================================

Input: LINE MouseDown(10,20) MouseDown(20,30) QUIT
Stack: **empty**
  terminate the program

Enable/Disable

The basic algorithm must be extended to support the enabling and disabling of devices. The enabling and disabling is always done just before any GetEvent is called. The following algorithm shows the necessary additions.

```
Push Start nonterminal on a stack
While Stack not empty do
  { S := Pop top symbol from stack;
  If (S is a terminal) then
    {Disable all devices;
    Enable(S);
    GetEvent(E);
    }
```

Else If (S is an action) then
   {DoCommand(S); }
Else If (S has only one production P) then
   { Push symbols of P on the stack in reverse order }
Else
   {Disable all devices;
   For each production P of S do
      { Enable(FirstSymbol(P)); }
   GetEvent(E)
   Select a production P using E
   Push all symbols in P, except the first one,
   onto the stack in reverse order.
   }
}

As with state machines the enabling and disabling can be optimized by first considering which devices are already enabled or disabled.

Contexts

Contexts are handled in much the same way as in recursive state machines. Certain nonterminals are defined as context nonterminals and a context definition (acquired device list and screen layout) is associated with each one. The dialog handling algorithm must be modified to handle the entry and exit from new contexts.

Push Start nonterminal on a stack
CurrentContext=Context(Start nonterminal);
AcquireAll(CurrentContext);
While Stack not empty do
   { S := Pop top symbol from stack;
   If (S is a terminal) then
      {..... }
   Else If (S is an action) then
      {DoCommand(S); }
   Else If (S is a nonterminal) then
      {If (S has a context) then
         {Push CurrentContext onto stack;
         ReleaseAll(CurrentContext);
         CurrentContext=Context(S);
         AcquireAll(CurrentContext);
         }

```
If (S has only one production P) then
    { Push symbols of P on the stack in
    reverse order }
Else
  {Disable all devices;
  For each production P of S do
      { Enable( FirstSymbol(P)); }
  GetEvent(E)
  Select a production P using E
  If (no production is selected) Then
      { .... }
  Else
      { .... }
  }
}
Else If (S is a context) then
  { ReleaseAll(CurrentContext);
  CurrentContext=S;
  AcquireAll(CurrentContext);
  }
}
```

One of the innovations of SYNGRAPH was automatic computation of a context's acquired device list. Each nonterminal in the grammar had a set of devices used which was defined as:

DevicesUsed(<NT>) = all logical devices found in the productions
    of <NT> plus the DevicesUsed of any
    nonterminal <N> which is not a new context
    that is found in the productions of <NT> .

In essence the algorithm recursively searches the productions and nonterminals looking for devices that are used without entering any nonterminals that themselves define new contexts.

Typed Picking

Another of the innovations in the SYNGRAPH system was the inclusion of typed picking of objects. When an object is drawn on the screen pick identifiers can be associated with them. In systems like CORE and GKS these pick identifiers are integers. When a pick device, such as a light pen or a locator, is used to select an object on the screen, the graphics package returns the pick identifier that is associated with the selected graphical image. The following figure shows a problem that arises when picking objects on the screen.

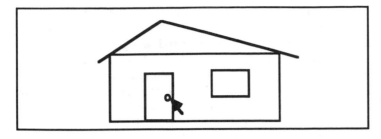

The object being picked in the above figure is ambiguous. It might be the house, the door, or the doorknob. This problem arises when objects are modeled as part hierarchies. SYNGRAPH's way of removing the ambiguity of such pick operations is to define a logical pick device for every type of object that can be picked. In our example these devices would be:

```
PickHouse = House;
PickDoor = Door;
PickKnob = Knob;
PickWindow = Window;
```

The user-defined types House, Door, and Knob are part of the semantic interface. Pick routines can then be defined that associate typed pick identifiers with every pickable object on the screen. The SYNGRAPH pick identifiers consist of a type indicator and a pointer to an object of the specified type. Thus a pick identifier is a direct reference to actual application data rather than an integer identifier that must be managed by the application. The following code shows how such identifiers would be supplied with the house shown above.

```
StartHousePick( PointerToHouse );
    .... draw the roof and walls ...
    StartWindowPick( PointerToWindow );
      .... draw the window
    EndPick;
    StartDoorPick( PointerToDoor );
      .... draw the door
      StartKnobPick( PointerToKnob );
          .... draw the knob
      EndPick;
    EndPick;
EndPick;
```

Note that SYNGRAPH maintains a stack of pick identifiers for each object rather than just one. The routines StartHousePick, StartWindowPick,

StartDoorPick, and StartKnobPick are generated as part of SYNGRAPH's semantic interface. Removing the picking ambiguity is handled through enabling and disabling of the logical pick devices. If a logical pick device is enabled then all images with pick identifiers of the corresponding type are pickable. Any image whose pick identifier corresponds to a disabled logical pick device cannot be selected. If, in the example shown above, the PickDoor input is the only one enabled then the picking is unambiguous. It is still possible for picking to be ambiguous if both PickDoor and PickHouse are enabled. In this case SYNGRAPH would start at the top of the pick stack and suggest a selection which the user could reject. SYNGRAPH would then move down the stack to a containing object.

Many interfaces consist of selecting a command by menu or function button and then selecting the arguments. In such a dialog this system would handle almost all picking ambiguity problems. In dialogs that select the object and then select the command, the logical pick devices could start productions having separate dialogs for each type of selected object. Such object/action dialogs would require all object selections to be unambiguous without relying on the type of the object.

Rub Out

One of the features found in many textual command interfaces is the ability to rub out inputs that were in error. In graphical interfaces the problem is what to do with the semantic actions that have already been executed, when a rub out occurs. In textual interfaces such facilities work because no semantics are executed until the command reaches closure, which is usually when a carriage return is entered. A similar capability can be added to a grammar UIMS.

The first problem is determining the scope for closure on a rub out. Rub out only applies to a limited section of the dialog at any one time and one can only back up so far. In SYNGRAPH the scope is determined by selected rub out nonterminals. Entering such a nonterminal marks the beginning of the scope and rub out cannot proceed back past this point. Leaving such a nonterminal indicates closure on the scope where all semantic actions are committed.

Recursive Descent Generation

Grammar dialog descriptions also lend themselves to direct implementation of the user interface in code. This technique is derived from recursive descent parser generation used in compiler construction. The basic idea is to generate a recursive procedure for every nonterminal in the grammar. The body of the procedure consists of the code necessary to parse the grammar. The generation algorithm proceeds as follows.

For each nonterminal in the grammar generate a recursive procedure with the same name as the nonterminal.

a. If the nonterminal defines a new context then generate code to save the current set of acquired devices, release all logical devices that are not part of the new context and acquire all logical devices that are part of the new context.

b. If the nonterminal has only one production then for each symbol of the production in order generate code as described below.

c. If the nonterminal has multiple productions then
  c.1. Generate code to enable only those logical devices which appear at the beginning of productions
  c.2. Generate a call to GetEvent
  c.3. Generate a case or switch statement based on on the logical device number which will select the correct production.
  c.4. For each production generate a branch of the case in the following form.
      for each symbol in the production except the first one generate code as described below

d. If the nonterminal defines a new context then generate code to restore the old context before returning.

Generation Algorithm for Production Symbols

d. If the symbol is a nonterminal then
  d.1. Generate a call to that nonterminal's procedure
  d.2. If the nonterminal defines a new context then generate the necessary acquire and release code to restore the current context after returning.

e. If the symbol is a terminal then
  e.1. Generate code to disable all logical devices and enable only the logical device indicated by the terminal
  e.2. Generate a call to GetEvent

f. If the symbol is an action then
  Generate the code to perform the action.

The following grammar can be used as an example to demonstrate how the generator would work.

```
<Dialog>[NewContext] ::= <Commands>
<Commands> ::=<Command> <Commands>
<Command> ::=
    LINE MouseDown [P1:=Evnt.MouseLoc]
      MouseDown [DrawLine(P1,Evnt.MouseLoc)]
    I RECTANGLE MouseDown [P1=Evnt.MouseLoc]
      MouseDown [DrawRect(P1,Evnt.MouseLoc) ]
    I ATTRIBUTES <AttributeMode>
<AttributeMode> [NewContext] ::= <AttrCmnd>
<AttrCmnd> ::= THICK [LineWidth=Thick] <AttrCmnd>
    I THIN [LineWidth=Thin] <AttrCmnd>
    I NOBORDER [ LineWidth = NoLine ] <AttrCmnd>
    I WHITE [Fill = White ] <AttrCmnd>
    I GRAY [Fill=Gray ] <AttrCmnd>
    I BLACK [Fill=Black ] <AttrCmnd>
    I RETURN
```

Given the grammar described above the following code might be generated for the nonterminals <Dialog> and <Command>.

```
void Dialog()
  {Context OldContext;

    SaveAcquiredDevices(OldContext);
    ReleaseAllDevices( );
    AcquireDevice(LINE);
    AcquireDevice(MouseDown);
    AcquireDevice(RECTANGLE);
    AcquireDevice(ATTRIBUTES);
    Commands( );
    RestoreContext(OldContext);
  }
void Command( )
  { Event Evnt;

    DisableAllDevices( );
    EnableDevice(LINE);
    EnableDevice(RECTANGLE);
    EnableDevice(ATTTRIBUTES);
    GetEvent(Evnt);
    switch (Evnt.LogicalDeviceCode) {
      LINE:
```

```
            DisableAllDevices; EnableDevice(MouseDown);
            GetEvent(Evnt);
            P1=Evnt.MouseLoc;
            DisableAllDevices;EnableDevice(MouseDown);
            GetEvent(Evnt);
            DrawLine(P1,Evnt.MouseLoc);
            break;
        RECTANGLE:
            DisableAllDevices;EnableDevice(MouseDown);
            GetEvent(Evnt);
            P1=Evnt.MouseLoc;
            DisableAllDevices;EnableDevice(MouseDown);
            GetEvent(Evnt);
            DrawRect(P1,Evnt.MouseLoc);
            break;
        ATTRIBUTES:
            AttributeMode();
            break
        }
    }
```

One of the advantages of a recursive descent implementation is that it is very easy to provide for attributes in the dialog description. The purpose of attributes is to propagate information from one part of the dialog to another. In the preceding example the DrawLine and DrawRect routines need to know the settings of LineWidth and Fill if they are to perform appropriately. In the technique shown above these values would have to be stored in global variables which is not a very good approach. We can provide for attributes by simply using the local variables and parameter mechanisms of the language that we are generating.

To provide for attributes we allow every nonterminal to have a parameter list and a set of local declarations. We also allow every nonterminal symbol to have an argument list. The example grammar would be transformed as follows.

```
<Dialog( )>[NewContext] ::= <Commands( )>
<Commands( )> ::=<Command(( )> <Commands( )>
<Command(( )> [long LineWidth=Thin;
    long FillCode=Black ] ::=
  LINE MouseDown [P1:=Evnt.MouseLoc]
    MouseDown[DrawLine(P1,Evnt.MouseLoc,Line
    Width,FillCode)]
```

```
   | RECTANGLE MouseDown [P1=Evnt.MouseLoc]
   MouseDown
   [DrawRect(P1,Evnt.MouseLoc,
        LineWidth,FillCode) ]
   | ATTRIBUTES <AttributeMode(&LineWidth, &FillCode)>

<AttributeMode(long *Width,long *Fill)>[NewContext]
   ::= <AttrCmnd(Width,Fill)>

<AttrCmnd(long *LineWidth,long *Fill)> ::=
   THICK[*LineWidth=Thick]<AttrCmnd(LineWidth,Fill)>
   | THIN[*LineWidth=Thin]<AttrCmnd(LineWidth,Fill)>
   | NOBORDER [ *LineWidth = NoLine ]
        <AttrCmnd(LineWidth,Fill)>
   | WHITE [*Fill = White ] <AttrCmnd(LineWidth,Fill)>
   | GRAY [*Fill=Gray ] <AttrCmnd(LineWidth,Fill)>
   | BLACK [*Fill=Black ] <AttrCmnd(LineWidth,Fill)>
   | RETURN
```

The generator is modified to generate the correct procedure and parameter declarations as well as the argument lists. The generated code for AttrCmnd would now be:

```
void AttrCmnd( LineWidth, Fill)
   long *LineWidth;
   long *Fill;
   { Event Evnt;

     DisableAllDevices( );
     EnableDevice(THICK);
     EnableDevice(THIN);
     EnableDevice(NOBORDER);
     EnableDevice(WHITE);
     EnableDevice(GRAY);
     EnableDevice(BLACK);
     EnableDevice(RETURN);
     GetEvent(Evnt);
     switch (Evnt.LogicalDeviceCode) {
       THICK
           *LineWidth=Thick;
           AttrCmnd(LineWidth,Fill);
           break;
```

```
THIN
    *LineWidth=Thin;
    AttrCmnd(LineWidth,Fill);
    break;
NOBORDER:
    *LineWidth=NoLine;
    AttrCmnd(LineWidth,Fill);
    break;
WHITE:
    *Fill=White;
    AttrCmnd(LineWidth,Fill);
    break;
GRAY:
    *Fill=Gray;
    AttrCmnd(LineWidth,Fill);
    break;
BLACK:
    *Fill=Black;
    AttrCmnd(LineWidth,Fill);
    break;
RETURN:
    break;
}
}
```

Attributes can be used in the state machine dialog models and in the table-driven implementations of grammars. In such cases the parse algorithms must be modified to handle the allocation and deallocation of space for attributes on an attribute stack, as well as the binding of attribute names to locations on the attribute stacks. Using the recursive descent technique the mechanisms already built into the programming language can perform these functions without additional work. A major drawback of the recursive descent approach is that it has a rather fixed sequencing mechanism which makes features like pervasive states or rub out more complicated to implement. SYNGRAPH used recursive descent to handle all of the semantics and attributes but used a state machine table for the dialog control. This hybrid architecture allowed rub out and escape mechanisms to be supported while using Pascal to handle the semantics.

Extended Grammars

Pure context-free grammars are somewhat awkward to use for programmers not familiar with formal languages. One of the most problematic features is the use of recursion instead of iteration. In the recursive descent implementation, recursion as a form of iteration is very expensive because of the large numbers of entries on the stack that can be generated. The interpretive grammar parser does not exhibit this problem but it still seems rather obscure to most programmers. Most grammar UIMSs have extended grammars to include more complex notations for productions. An example would be to use curly braces to indicate sections that should be repeated zero or more times and to use parentheses to build up sub expressions. For example,

<Dialog> ::= { (<Line> | <Rectangle> | <Attributes) } QUIT

This example indicates that a dialog consists of zero or more Line, Rectangle, or Attributes commands, followed by QUIT. Such extensions are equivalent to recursive state machines and are usually converted from an external grammar dialog description to an internal state machine description for run time execution.

Summary of Grammar UIMSs

Grammars provide essentially the same capabilities as state machines. This is true both of the personnel roles that the model supports and the portions of the UIMS architecture that they address. They do have the advantage of implicitly defining states in a sequence but for some reason they are harder for programmers to understand as a programming rather than as a descriptive medium. The ability to easily specify sequences of inputs has a tendency to lead designers toward long sequences which are, in general, not good dialog design. The important concepts that were developed for grammars are recursive descent generation, picking of typed objects, and rub out. The last two ideas are applicable to state machine models.

References

1 Hanau, P.R. and D.R. Lenorovitz. *Prototypeing and Simulation Tools for User/Computer Dialogue Design.* **Computer Graphics** 14(3), August 1980.

2 Olsen, D.R. and E. P. Dempsey. *SYNGRAPH: A Graphical User Interface Generator.* **Computer Graphics** 17(3), July 1983.

5.
Event-based UIMSs

The state machine and grammar dialog models interpret the meaning of the user's inputs based on the current state of the dialog. Such interpretation is known as sequential demultiplexing of inputs. The meaning of a given input is determined by where it occurs in the sequence of inputs. Since direct manipulation interfaces have become popular it has become more important to provide spatial demultiplexing of inputs. The meaning of the input is determined by the visual object or window at which the input is directed. Spatial demultiplexing leads interface designers towards a "What visual item am I interacting with now?" point of view, while sequential demultiplexing leads to a "What is legal to do next?" point of view.

This chapter will review several related models for attaching interactive behavior to visual objects displayed on the screen. The MENULAY system was an early approach to attaching actions to images. Later windowing systems have provided event translations for mapping events directed at windows on the screen to specific semantic actions. Object- oriented systems have taken the event-mapping concepts and placed them in a programming language framework that allows reuse of interactive fragments along with a more easily understood message-handling mechanism. HyperCard brings object-oriented concepts back into a visual interface design metaphor similar to MENULAY.

MENULAY

This early UIMS, created by Buxton and coworkers,[1] turned away from the input processing models of other UIMS architectures and adopted screen layout drawings as its basic dialog metaphor instead. To create an interface the designer first draws how the screen should appear to the end user. This drawing is done using a graphical editor. The drawing is segmented into icons, which can be any image at all. Each of these icons can then be given a selection event and a semantic action to be used when the icon is selected. Take, for example, the interface to a simple chemistry problem given in figure 5:1.

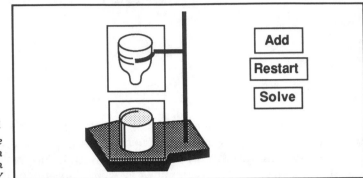

Fig. 5:1
*Interface
Design
with
MENULAY*

The burette, beaker, and command names are each separate icons to which actions can be attached. Each such screen drawing is stored as a table of interaction item entries. Each item entry consists of the icon's graphical primitives, XY extent, selection event code, address of the semantic function to be called, and any parameters for that semantic function.

At run time the internal dialog description consists of one or more screen definitions. One of them is the current screen as shown in figure 5:2.

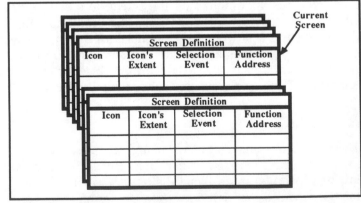

Fig. 5:2
*MENULAY
Interface
Tables*

The dialog management algorithm is simple:

```
Repeat
    GetEvent ( E )
    For each item I in CurrentScreen
        If (E.MouseLoc is inside of I.IconExtent)
            and (E.EventCode = I.SelectEvent) then
        Invoke I.SemanticAction with I.Parameters

Until Quit
```

Further control of the user interface is possible by calling a library of routines which will do such chores as draw on the screen, change the current screen definition, or move some of the icon locations.

The primary advantage of the MENULAY model is its simplicity. One draws a picture of the user interface, attaches active regions to the picture in the form of icons, and then associates a semantic action and parameters with each such icon. The model used for designing interfaces is intuitive to people who are thinking visually about how the interface should appear. The simplicity of the MENULAY model is also its largest drawback. First, there is the awkwardness of building large interfaces as a finite set of screens, each with a flat structure and no abstraction facilities. Secondly, there is the lack of any syntactic or sequential knowledge at all, which is universal for event systems. This particular deficiency will be discussed later.

Window Systems

The advent of overlapping window systems has also lead to event handlers that have some of the properties of a UIMS. Most notably they contain the notion of external control, where the window system calls the application when some interactive service is required. Such systems also have limited external dialog descriptions.

The Window Environment

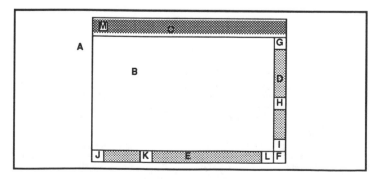

Fig. 5:3

Sample
Window
Layout

For purposes of this discussion we will consider windowing systems that allow for windows inside windows, as shown in figure 5:3.

This group of windows forms the tree shown in figure 5:4.

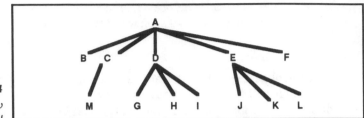

Because the windows overlap they are arranged in back to front order with the parent window always lying behind its children. We can consider each window as an interactive object with its own behavior. Due to the nature of windowing systems, each window is responsible for redrawing itself whenever part of the window becomes damaged because of the movements of other windows. This same mechanism of getting the application to perform the redraw can also be used for other kinds of events.

When an interactive event arrives we decide what to do with it based on the window in which the mouse location lies currently. The rule is to pick the lowest, front most window in the tree whose extent contains the mouse location. This rule has the obvious effect of picking whichever window the mouse appears to be pointing at. The problem then remains to map the event to some application action that should be performed.

Translation Tables

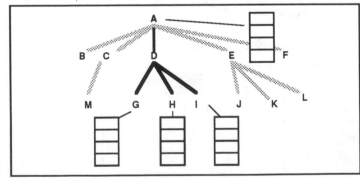

Fig. 5:5

*Window
Hierarchy with
Event Tables*

Translation tables are a basic mechanism for handling events directed at

windows. One of the first published uses of translation tables was in the GIGO/Canvas system.[2] In this system each interactive event is characterized by an integer event code. Each window has an associated translation table as shown in figure 5:5.

The tables are indexed by event number. Each entry in the table contains the address of a procedure that will handle the event. An event procedure is passed the window which was selected and the event record. It may then perform whatever semantic actions are desired. More than one window may share an event table so as to save space and construction time.

The dialog-handling algorithm is:

```
GetEvent(E);
Find the lowest, front most, visible window W which contains
    MousePosition(E)
    Invoke the routine at W.EventTable[E.EventCode] passing
    W and E as parameters.
```

This algorithm was also included, with some extensions, in the SunView Notifier which handles input events on Sun workstations.

The X-Windows toolkit provides a similar set of features. Each of the semantic routines is registered with the toolkit as follows.

```
XtActionsRec Actions[]={
    {"Click",Click},
    {"DoubleClick",DoubleClick},
    {"Delete",Delete},
    {"Hilight",Highlight},
    }
XtAppAddActions( Actions,4);
```

This simply attaches textual names to procedure addresses. These names are then used in a translation table specification.

```
char *Translate=
    "<Btn1Down>: Click() \n\
    <Btn1Down><Btn1Up><Btn1Down>: \
    DoubleClick()\n\
    <Key>D:Delete() \n\
    <EnterWindow>: Hilight(On)\n\
    <LeaveWindow>:Hilight(Off)";
XtParseTranslationTable(Translate);
```

The actual structure of X translation tables is hidden from the users. A string is passed to XtParseTranslationTable which converts the external description to an appropriate internal one. The translation table parsing has been designed so that the translation table can be either defined inside the C code of the application or read from an external description file. Note that the sequence <Btn1Down> <Btn1Up><Btn1Down> has been mapped to the DoubleClick action. This limited form of event sequencing is provided in the toolkit but the semantics are not well defined.

Pseudo Events and Event Promotion

Two extensions to this basic event model increase its functionality. The first is the concept of a pseudo event. The system event codes only account for a small number of possible events. If there are 256 event codes, typically, less than 20 of them will be used to handle interactive events. The remaining codes can be allocated for other purposes by the application. The windowing system can then provide a PseudoEvent routine that will accept an artificial event and a window to which it should be directed. The PseudoEvent routine simply invokes the correct routine in the translation table based on the event code in the PseudoEvent. This primitive mechanism for communication between windows can be quite useful.

An important use of pseudo events is event promotion. A standard routine takes an event and sends it to the parent window of the window that received the event. In some systems this promotion routine is the default action for all event codes. The fundamental idea is that a window should handle any events that it can and forward others on to its parent.

Matching versus Indexing

In the preceding discussion the correct event routine to call was determined by using the event code as an index into the table of events. This use of the event code has the advantage of being very fast and simple to implement. A problem arises, however, when there are various modifier keys or other conditions that might control the meaning of the event. For example, a button press may mean something different if the shift key is pressed simultaneously. One possibility is to enumerate all possible combinations of modifiers. This approach becomes a problem if one wants meta-control-C to specify a particular command. An alternative approach is to simply specify a pattern to be matched in the event record and then associate a routine with each such pattern. This approach requires that the event be successively matched against each pattern, and invoking the one that matches, which has some performance problems. Optimizations of this approach will be discussed in the next chapter.

Event Delegation Procedures

An alternative strategy is to associate a handler procedure with each window. This is the strategy used in Microsoft Windows. When any event occurs in that window, the handler procedure is called and passed a pointer to the event record. The handler procedure is then responsible for checking the event code and performing the appropriate action. A handler procedure can then send any event to itself or any other window for which it has a pointer.

The delegation notion comes from the common use of predefined event handlers. Suppose that a handler procedure had been written for scroll bars. This procedure would accept the pseudo events, NewMax, NewMin, and NewCurrent. Whenever this procedure moved the scroll bar it would send its own window the NewCurrent event. By itself the scroll bar handler doesn't do anything except move the scroll bar up and down. If we wanted to tie this scroll bar to a text window we could write a new handler procedure which would take each event received and delegate it to the scroll bar handler. After the scroll bar handler is done, this new handler could check to see if the event was a NewCurrent event. If it was, then this message could be forwarded to the text window as a NewVScroll event. The new handler delegates most interactions to the scroll bar handler and provides only the "glue" operations to tie the scroll bar to the text window.

Object-oriented Event Systems

The assembly of translation tables and pseudo events can become cumbersome. In addition, there are many functions that various window handlers have in common. An alternative approach to building translations by hand is to use an object-oriented system with inheritance. Only the barest rudiments of object-oriented programming will be discussed here so as to emphasize the interaction problems.

Object-oriented Systems

In an object-oriented system an object consists of data and a class that defines how those data are to be used. The nature of the data varies from system to system in how it is stored and used. A class consists of some definition of the data and some methods that can be used on the data. In general, only the methods are visible to users of the class. A method is simply a procedure that is unique to that class. One operates on objects by sending them messages. A message consists of the name of the method to be invoked and the arguments to be passed. In most systems the sending of a message simply invokes the corresponding method procedure. Object-oriented messages are not to be confused with operating system messages between processes, although they may be used as such. In most object-oriented systems an object is characterized by its class and a class is characterized by the methods that are defined on it.

Object-oriented Interaction

The simplest use of object-oriented programming is to define a message for each input event. The application defines classes that accept those messages and perform the necessary semantic actions. A user interface is defined by attaching an object to each window. When an event is directed to a particular window, the windowing package sends the corresponding message to the window's object. In this model the object system takes over the functions that were handled by the translation tables. The advantage of the object-oriented approach is that the whole event-handling process is naturally integrated with the programming language.

Inheritance

One of the primary advantages of object-oriented systems is the notion of inheritance. Take, for example, a class ScrollBar which implements the scroll bar shown in figure 5:6.

Fig. 5:6
Horizontal
Scroll Bar

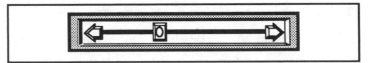

This class could have the following methods.

```
Class ScrollBar Superclass = Object;
  {MouseDown(MouseX,MouseY)
    /* Called when the mouse button is pressed.
    Checks to see where in the scroll bar it was pressed
    and performs the appropriate operation. */
  MouseUp(MouseX,MouseY)
    /* Called when the mouse button is released.
    Modifies the value of the slider. */
  Redraw(TheWindow);
    /* Called by the window system to redraw the scroll bar. */
  ChangeScrollValue(NewValue);
    /*Called by the application to change the
    scroll bar's value. */
```

```
ChangeRange(Min,Max);
    /*Called by the application to change the
    scroll bar's range. */
UpdateScrollVal(NewValue);
    /*Called by the MouseUp method to notify the application
    that the scroll bar has changed. */
}
```

The first three methods interface with the window system. The last three methods interface with the application. When using this scroll bar implementation the only thing that must change between uses is the behavior of UpdateScrollVal which actually does the semantic changing. All the rest of the implementation can stay the same.

The technique for reusing such code is inheritance. We can define a new class which has ScrollBar as its superclass. We then redefine the method UpdateScrollVal and add any new methods that this application of ScrollBar might need. As an example, consider a scroll bar that scrolls a drawing back and forth within a window. We might define the following class.

```
Class HorizontalWindowScroll Superclass= ScrollBar;
    { SetWindow( Window )
        /* Sets the window that is to be scrolled. */
    SetWidth( Width )
        /* Sets the width of the world coordinates to be
        scrolled across. */
    UpdateScrollVal( NewValue );
        /* Set the X coordinate of the window's origin
        based on the new scroll value. */
    }
```

In the class HorizontalWindowScroll all of ScrollBar methods are inherited and function as before, with the exception of UpdateScrollVal which has been redefined inside HorizontalWindowScroll. In addition, the method SetWidth has been defined to simplify the setting of the range of scrolling. By telling HorizontalWindowScroll what the total width of world coordinates is the range can be calculated and ChangeRange invoked to do the actual setting. Using a scroll bar to scroll across world coordinates is not as simple as setting the range to run from zero to Width. The current width of the window must be taken into account. The advantage of the object-oriented approach is that HorizontalWindowScroll need only concern itself with the issues of windows and their scrolling problems. The superclass ScrollBar automatically handles the user interface issues. The superclass-subclass relationship is very similar to the event-delegation approach described earlier, except that it has better programming language support.

MacApp

Apple discovered that programming the Macintosh toolbox was a difficult problem for many programmers and a tedious one for all programmers. The difficulty was not because of major flaws in the toolbox design but rather because user interface programming is a hard problem. To alleviate this they developed MacApp.[3] MacApp is based on Object Pascal which is a single inheritance object-oriented language. MacApp consists of a standard Macintosh application preprogrammed with the normal event loop, window, and menu handling strategies.

The advantage of the MacApp approach is that the interactive application is already written. The problem is how to modify this program to accommodate the specific application the programmer is working on. This process of modifying MacApp for a particular application is one of specializing the general program to fit the current specific need. The kinds of items that need specialization include the menus, actual window behavior, dialog box functions, and layouts. MacApp's approach is to define general classes for each such item with all of the normal user interface processing programmed into them. Such general classes are very much like the ScrollBar class described above. The application programmer then defines subclasses of these general classes much like the HorizontalWindowScroll example. In these subclasses the programmer can use or override as little or as much of the standard functionality as desired.

X Widgets

The X toolkit[4] provides an object-oriented mechanism for handling events and other user interface issues. The basic user interface construction mechanism is the widget class. A widget class defines a class of interactive behaviors that take place inside a particular X window. The horizontal scroll bar would be an example of such a widget class. A window with scroll bars at the sides and a drawing area in the middle would be a composite widget class. The application program can create instances of a widget class such as a particular window or scroll bar.

A widget class defines its own data structure for storing information and defines a set of resources which the application can set in that data structure. A resource is simply a named piece of information that the widget needs in order to function. In the scroll bar example one might define resources for the color of the bar, the color of the slider knob, or, perhaps, the icon to be used for the arrowheads. Each widget class has a resource list which specifies the textual names, resource types, offsets in the widget record, and other information that helps the resource manager know what kind of resources the widget will need.

Every widget class has a superclass from which it can inherit resource values. In addition, when a widget class is instantiated to create a specific widget, an argument list can be provided which can set the values of some of the widget resources. In general, the value of a widget's resource gives first priority to any argument list value for that resource. If there is no argument list setting then it looks in the resource database under the widget's class. If there is no entry for the resource under the widget's class, then it searches up the superclass hierarchy for a value for that resource. If the superclass chain does not yield a value, then it will use the default value defined for the widget class itself.

A particular installation of X-Windows can have a textual resource file defined for it which associates values with resource names. The resource names can be specialized by widget class. In addition, each application can have its own associated resource file. Application resource definitions override the overall definitions. When a widget is instantiated, all of the databases, superclasses, and argument lists are searched to find the resource values before the widget begins executing.

One special kind of resource is the callback list. A widget defines a callback resource for each action that the widget needs the application to perform. Such a resource has a callback list of application routines to be invoked when such a need arises. In our scroll bar example, ChangeScrollValue, ChangeRange, and UpdateScrollVal would each be represented as a callback list resource. The purpose of a list, instead of a single callback, is to allow multiple actions to be invoked if desirable. In addition to callbacks, each widget has a translation table which maps interactive inputs to specific widget routines to handle them. These routines can be either defined in the widget or inherited from the widget's superclass. It is the translation actions that will call the various callbacks when application intervention is required.

Our scroll bar example can be used to demonstrate the interrelationship between translation tables, resources, and callback lists. In a scroll bar widget there might be a PageWidth resource, a callback list resource for UpdateScrollVal, and a translation table entry for mouse presses which is mapped to the widget routine MouseDown. If the mouse button event is pressed while over the slider area to the left of the thumb then the translation table entry would be searched and the widget routine MouseDown would be invoked. MouseDown would detect the location of the event and interpret its interactive meaning as scroll back one page width. Based on the location of the event, MouseDown might fetch the resource value of PageWidth, subtract it from the current scroll bar value, move the thumb to the appropriate location on the slider, and then invoke the UpdateScrollVal callback to inform the application of what has happened.

The widget class mechanism of the X toolkit is a good deal more complicated than has been described here. The X toolkit has a number of competing mechanisms and the interrelationships are not all clear. The widget class mechanism does provide for abstracting interactive behavior and for inheriting information via a superclass mechanism. The event-dispatching mechanism is a simple translation table.

HyperCard

An alternative approach pursued at Apple, and since then by other software houses, combines the graphical form of interface design exemplified by MENULAY with the object- oriented approach for event handling. The result is HyperCard[5] and other related systems.

Basic HyperCard Concepts

A HyperCard program is called a stack. The model for such programs is a stack of 3 by 5 cards. Each stack has several backgrounds and each card has a particular background. A background behaves very much like a card except that the items on a background can be shared by multiple cards. A card or a background can be drawn on in much the same fashion as MENULAY except that the painting facilities are much more advanced. In addition, cards and backgrounds can have buttons and/or fields placed on them. A button is simply a location that can be clicked on to invoke some behavior. A variety of button styles can be selected as shown in figure 5:7. Button behavior will be described later.

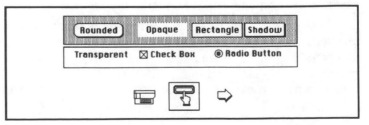

Fig. 5:7

Sample HyperCard Buttons

A field is a rectangular area in which text can be edited. There are a variety of field presentations that can be selected, as shown in figure 5:8. The text which a user can enter into a field is stored with the card, even if the field is drawn on the background. This arrangement allows a standard set of fields to be laid out on a background with multiple cards sharing that background, each with its own information.

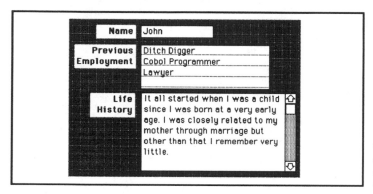

Fig. 5:8

Sample HyperCard Fields

The labels shown with the field are part of the painting on the card and are only visually associated with the fields.

Event Handling

Having drawn a set of cards and backgrounds, the interface designer needs to define the interactive behavior of the user interface. These definitions are specified via HyperTalk scripts. These scripts can be attached to buttons, fields, cards, backgrounds, and stacks. There is also a script attached to the HyperCard program itself.

HyperTalk

HyperTalk is a textual event language. The design of HyperTalk was an attempt to be English-like. This has not succeeded totally since it is a programming language with corresponding needs, which are different from English. The language is structured around the sending of events. Figure 5:9 shows an example HyperTalk script.

```
on mouseUp
  global PreviousName
  put field "Name" into PreviousName
  PurgeName
end mouseUp
on PurgeName
  put "???" into field "Name"
end PurgeName
```

The "on" statement specifies what to do when a particular event occurs. In the sample script the standard event "mouseUp" is being handled. For all the interactive events that can occur a standard HyperTalk event name is defined. The special "global" statement defines a global variable and the "put" statement performs assignments between various containers such as variables and fields. A variety of other special event names have been defined to perform textual editing on fields, graphical drawing on cards, and creation and deletion of cards. The philosophy of HyperTalk is that anything that can be done interactively though the HyperCard interface will also have a corresponding HyperTalk event that can perform the same function in a similar manner. In addition to the predefined events, the interface designer can define new events by specifying an "on" statement for that event. The event "PurgeName" is an example of such an event. Designer-defined events are invoked and used exactly like the built in events. Events can also have parameters defined for them which makes them very much like procedures.

Inheritance

Scripts are attached to buttons, fields, cards, backgrounds, stacks, and HyperCard itself. The handling of an event is controlled by an inheritance path defined on these items. Figure 5:10 shows the HyperCard inheritance path.

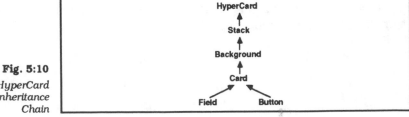

Fig. 5:10
HyperCard Inheritance Chain

When a field script does not have an "on" statement for a given event, the event is forwarded to the current card. If the card does not have the event it is forwarded on up the chain, searching for a script that can handle the event. If an event reaches the top of the chain without finding a handler then an error is reported. The goal of this inheritance structure is more the sharing of event handlers across various HyperCard pieces than the reuse of existing code. The inheritance chain is fixed rather than defined by the superclass structure of normal object-oriented languages.

In addition to the event inheritance, each card can inherit the graphics, buttons, and fields of its background. Visually, this is an overlay process. The background graphic image is drawn, followed by the buttons and fields of the background, the graphic image of the card, and, finally, the buttons and fields of the card. Each successive layer may obscure the layers previously drawn.

Internal Structure

A HyperCard stack consists of a set of backgrounds and a set of cards. Each card has a background, a graphic image, a list of buttons, and a list of fields. Figure 5:11 shows this structure.

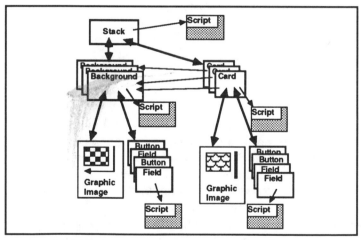

Fig. 5:11
HyperCard Stack Structure

This structure drives HyperCard's event-handling algorithm.

Event-handling Algorithm

The event-handling algorithm is driven entirely by the current card. There is a HyperTalk event that will change the current card. The event-handling process is to take the mouse location of the input event and determine which field or button the mouse was inside when the event occurred. This will determine where the event should be sent. If two or more fields or buttons overlap, then the event is sent to the front most one. If the event does not lie in any button or field, then the event is sent to the card. The entire algorithm, including inheritance, is shown in figure 5:12.

Fig. 5:12
HyperCard Event Handling

```
While not QuittingTime
  { GetEvent(E);
  Item = FindSelectedFieldOrButton(CurrentCard);
  If Item isn't NULL Then
    { EventHandled = HandleEvent(E,Item.Script) }
  else
    {Event Handled = False }
  If not EventHandled Then
    {If not HandleEvent(E,CurrentCard.Script)Then
      {If not HandleEvent(E,
            CurrentCard.Background.Script)Then
        {If not HandleEvent(E,Stack.Script) Then
          {If notHandleEvent(E,HyperCard.Script)Then
            { display error message }
          }
        }
      }
    }
  }
```

Extensibility

HyperTalk has two main problems. First, it is interpretive which makes it rather slow. Secondly, it is not a full programming language with data structures and other amenities suitable for programming. To accommodate this need the notion of XCMDs has been added. An XCMD is simply a Macintosh code resource. There are special facilities in most Macintosh compilers for creating such code resources.

The algorithm in figure 5:12 is modified so that if an event is not found in the stack's script, then the resources of the stack are checked for an XCMD resource whose name matches the event name. If one is found then the parameters are passed to that code as a string. If one is not found then the search continues on to HyperCard's script as before. A number of routines are provided that an XCMD can call, which will set fields or perform other HyperCard functions from inside an XCMD. This facility does allow HyperCard to be extended to invoke arbitrary application code but the mechanisms are rather clumsy and require the careful work of an expert programmer.

Summary of Event Handling

The event-handling approach to user interface management is based on two fundamental ideas. First, the interface should be defined not in terms of syntax or states but in terms of the visual objects that appear on the screen. Secondly, after an object has been identified to which an event should be sent, there is a direct mapping from events to semantic actions. These two concepts give us highly visual, free-form user interfaces with a simply explained dialog-handling mechanism. The object-oriented strategies also provide us with a mechanism for encapsulating user interface behavior which can be reused without knowing the detailed implementation.

There is, however, a basic problem with syntax. Take, for example, the layout for the simple drawing package shown in figure 5:13.

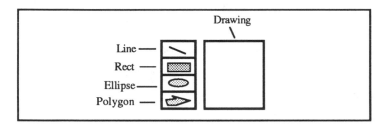

Fig. 5:13
Simple Drawing Application

For exposition, each of the active icons has been labeled. The syntax problem arises when the end user clicks on the Line icon and then wants to draw in the Drawing region. Recognizing the click on Line is easy. Recognizing a MouseDown event inside Drawing is also easy. But when MouseDown occurs in Drawing, does it signify that a rubber line, a rubber rectangle, or a rubber ellipse should be echoed? When the MouseUp occurs inside Drawing, should a line be created or should the echoing continue if a polygon has not been closed? Even in this simple, spatially oriented application there is some level of sequential syntax for which this model does not account. It is the semantic action routines that must track the current state of the interface and handle any of the syntactic issues. The event model provides no support for such interactive problems. This approach essentially eliminates the dialog control component by passing events directly from the lexical handler (or in many cases the graphics package) to the application code.

The forced inclusion of portions of the syntax in the application code also violates some of the intent for which UIMS work was begun. When portions of the syntax are in code, the dialog author must be a programmer. This approach also eliminates the dialog description from the UIMS architecture.

In spite of these deficiencies, the event-handler approach has achieved a dominant position in terms of actual usage because of its simplicity and ability to associate behavior directly with visual objects. This association of behavior with what the user sees rather than with some internal state is a major improvement over the models discussed so far. While these systems provide poor support for dialog authors, they can provide excellent support for graphics designers. The success of HyperCard is largely due to the tight coupling of the visual objects to the activities to be performed.

References

1 Buxton, W., M.R. Lamb, D. Sherman, and K.C. Smith. *Towards a Comprehensive User Interface Management System.* **Computer Graphics** 17(3): 35-42, July 1983.

2 Rosenthal, D.S.H. *Managing Graphical Resources.* **Computer Graphics** 17(1): 38-45, January 1983.

3 Schmucker, K.J. **Object-Oriented Programming for the Macintosh.** Hasbrouck Heights, NJ: Hayden Book Company, 1986.

4 McCormack, J. and P. Asente. *Using the X Toolkit or How to Write a Widget.* **Proceedings USENIX Summer 1988 Conference**, 1988.

5 Goodman, D. **The Complete HyperCard Handbook.** New York: Bantam Books, 1987.

6.
Production Systems

In the preceding chapters we have discussed syntactic models for dialogs as well as visual and window-based models. Each has its strengths and weaknesses. The primary problem with the syntactic models is that the definition of the dialog is divorced from the visual objects being manipulated. The primary problem with visual models is that they have no notion of syntactic issues such as ordered sequences. We can resolve this deficiency of the visual model by placing a recursive state machine on each window. The state machine is a superset of the translation table. This addition resolves the syntax problems of window event systems. In many cases the state machines become trivial since most of the meaning of inputs is decoded spatially rather than sequentially.

There are, however, three unresolved problems. First, state machines can be too ordered, even when different machines are associated with each of various windows. Secondly, there is no communication between the state machines associated with various windows in the hierarchy. Thirdly, the state machine model does not permit a notion of inheritance which allows previously designed interactions to be reused and enhanced without modifying them. Many of the event-handler systems have such a notion of inheritance.

To understand how a state machine can be too ordered, consider a semantic command that requires three inputs, A, B, and C. Suppose that

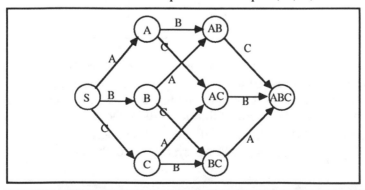

Fig. 6:1
Handling
Unordered
Inputs

each of these inputs should be entered only once and the order in which they are entered is unimportant. Figure 6:1 shows a state machine to handle this case.

The simple problem of entering N inputs in any order by this strategy requires 2^N states. An alternative solution, without so many states, is shown in figure 6:2.

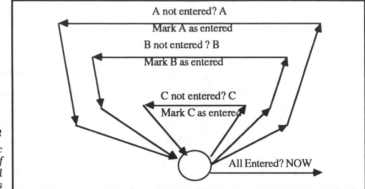

Fig. 6:2

The Semantic Handling of Unordered Inputs

The approach in figure 6:2 handles the problem of unordered inputs but again forces syntactic concepts into the application code. People understand what each action and each guard means by reading the labels, but our algorithms know them only as procedure addresses and cannot exploit or understand such implicit meanings. Forcing syntactic concepts into the application code also violates our goal of keeping dialog issues out of the application as much as possible.

To illustrate the need for communication between machines, consider again the case of the drawing program shown in figure 6:3.

Fig. 6:3

Simple Drawing

When the window containing the rectangle icon is selected the drawing window's state machine must be informed so that it can know what kind of dialog to use in responding to its own mouse inputs. In addition, the line icon window needs to be informed that it should remove its highlight.

The remainder of this chapter will discuss the Event Response Language (ERL) used in the SASSAFRAS system[1] and the Propositional

---

Production Systems (PPS)[2] which is a later production system model. These systems are based on a set of productions that have a left-hand side which tests for a set of conditions, and a right-hand side which is a set of conditions that should be asserted. In many respects a rule is similar to a state transition except that the single state/single transition restriction is removed.

Event Response Language

The Event Response Language is based on input events, which are received by a module, flags, which are internal to a module, and output events, which are sent by a module. Input and output events can have value fields associated with them. An example input event would be MouseDown which would have X and Y as its value fields. Flags are simply named conditions that can be *raised*.

The major portion of the dialog specification is a set of rules. Each rule has the form:

> *condition -> action*

A condition may be an input event with a list of flags, or simply a list of flags. Rules with no input events in their conditions are called ε-rules. The action part of a rule consists of sending output events, raising flags, and making assignments to event fields. Figure 6:4 contains sample ERL rules.

Fig. 6:4
Sample ERL Rules

```
1. MouseDown waitingForLine ->
   StartLine.X <- MouseDown.X
   StartLine.Y <- MouseDown.Y
   StartLine !
   lineDragging ^
2. MouseDown waitingForCircle ->
   CircleCenter.X <- MouseDown.X
   CircleCenter.Y <- MouseDown.Y
   CircleCenter !
   circleDragging ^
3. MouseUp circleDragging ->
   EnterCircle.X <- MouseUp.X
   EnterCircle.Y <- MouseUp.Y
   EnterCircle !
   waitingForCircle ^
```

Rule 1 in figure 6:4 fires whenever the MouseDown event occurs while the flag waitingForLine is raised. Rule 2 fires if the waitingForCircle flag is raised. It is possible that both rules 1 and 2 might fire on MouseDown if both waitingForLine and waitingForCircle are raised. Such multiple actions on a single event can be very useful, although in this particular example such a situation would probably indicate a programming error. In rule 1 the assignments transfer values from the input event to the StartLine output event. The statement StartLine! actually sends the event. The last thing that rule 2 does is raise the flag circleDragging. By raising this flag it becomes possible for rule 3 to fire when MouseUp occurs.

The semantic interface is handled by output events such as StartLine, CircleCenter, and EnterCircle. Output events need not be semantic constructs; they could be sent to other ERL modules to control other parts of the user interface. These communication issues will be discussed later.

Flags are the primary control mechanism for defining syntax in ERL. The flags waitingForCircle and circleDragging handle the syntax of entering the center and radius points of the circle. Such flags add the necessary control to the dialog model that was lacking in simple event handlers. Flags that appear in the condition of a rule that fires are lowered after the rule fires. Such flags can be raised again but this must be explicitly done in the action part of the rule.

ERL can also solve the unordered input problem discussed earlier. The rules necessary to solve this are shown in figure 6:5.

Fig. 6:5

ERL solution to unordered input

```
StartInputs ->
    needA^ needB^ needC^
InputA needA ->
    .SaveA <- InputA.Value
    haveA^
InputB needB ->
    .SaveB <- InputB.Value
    haveB^
InputC needC ->
    .SaveC <- InputC.Value
    haveC^
haveA haveB haveC ->
    DoAction.A <- .SaveA
    DoAction.B <- .SaveB
    DoAction.C <- .SaveC
    DoAction !
```

The ERL implementation of unordered input requires only one additional rule for each input. Instead of tracking inputs as part of the application semantics or in multiple states, flags are used to remember which inputs have been received.

The algorithm for evaluating ERL specifications is shown in figure 6:6.

Fig. 6:6

```
{ FireableRules = True;
While FireableRules Do
  { FireableRules = False;
  For each ε-rule R do
    { If all of the flags in R.condition are raised then
      {Mark R as fireable;
      FireableRules = True;
      }
    else
      { Mark R as not fireable; }
    }
  For each ε-rule R which is fireable do
    { lower all flags in R.condition }
  For each ε-rule R which is fireable do
    { execute R.action }
  }
GetEvent(E);
For each event rule R do
  { If all of the flags in R.condition are raised
          and E matches R.Event then
    {Mark R as fireable;
    }
  else
    { Mark R as not fireable; }
  }
For each rule R which is fireable do
  { lower all flags in R.condition }
For each rule R which is fireable do
  { execute R.action }
}
```

The first part of the algorithm processes all of the rules that do not have events in their conditions. These rules are similar to the NOW transitions defined for state machines. They do not depend on input events for them to fire. Processing all e-rules first and repeatedly is essential since the flags raised in one rule's action may cause another e-rule to become fireable.

Communication Mechanisms in SASSAFRAS

An essential component of SASSAFRAS is the Local Event Broadcast Mechanism. This is the mechanism for communicating between ERL modules and between the dialog modules, input modules, and application modules. For communication, modules are grouped into clusters. All module output events (such as the EnterCircle event) are sent to the cluster controller. The cluster controller queues the event for processing.

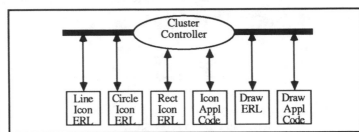

Fig. 6:7
Example LEBM
Architecture

When an event is removed from the queue the cluster controller checks each module to see which ones want the event. Any module that can accept the event then executes until it has completed handling the event. Any newly produced events are placed in the queue.

Given the simple drawing application in figure 6:3 we can define six ERL modules: one each for the line, circle, and rectangle icons; one for the drawing window; one for the icon-handling application code; and one for the drawing application code. This architecture is shown in figure 6:7.

When the line icon module receives a MouseDown event in its window, it broadcasts the LineSelected and IconSelected events. The icon application module accepts the IconSelected event and changes the highlighted icon to the line icon. The draw window module receives the LineSelected event and sets its waitingForLine flag which gives meaning to any subsequent mouse events sent to that window.

In order to handle sequencing problems a cluster controller has an external and internal queue. Events generated within the modules of the cluster are placed in the internal queue, while events coming from outside the cluster are placed in the external queue. The external queue is accessed only when the internal queue is empty. The reason for the two queues is so that internal events can be used to allow modules to cooperate in handling some external event completely, before beginning processing on the next external event.

Propositional Production Systems

A Propositional Production System (PPS) is a superset of state machines, translation tables, and ERL. The name is derived from the fact that the reasoning involved is equivalent to propositional logic. In addition, a PPS is formally equivalent to finite state machines and regular grammars. A PPS can succinctly describe systems that would be tedious to describe in other models of the same power.

There are three attributes of a PPS that are particularly applicable to the problem of handling graphical dialogs. A PPS can:

1. Enable and disable events.
2. Support semantic conditions such as not allowing a Save command to be performed when there is no file open.
3. Inherit behavior from one or more PPS definitions.

Our discussion of a PPS consists of four parts: 1) definition of PPSs and certain operations that can be performed on them; 2) dialog processing algorithms; 3) relationships to three of the other models of input handling; and 4) a set of automatic optimizations that increase evaluation speed.

Basic Definition of a PPS

A Propositional Production System consists of a state space definition and a set of rules. A state space is characterized by a set of conditions much like the events and flags in ERL, or the states and inputs in state machines. Conditions are grouped in fields with all conditions in a given field being mutually exclusive. Take the example of a simple drawing application shown in figure 6:8.

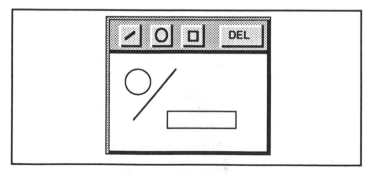

Fig. 6:8
Sample
Drawing

The state space for such an application might be represented as shown in figure 6:9.

State Space for Sample Drawing Application

>Field ActiveCmnd (NoCmnd,LineCmnd,CircleCmnd,RectCmnd)
>Semantic Field SelectedObj (NoSelection,LineSel,CircleSel,RectSel)
>Field DragMode(RubberLine,RubberCircle,RubberRect,DragSelect, NotDragging)
>Query Field ConfirmDel(OKDelete, CancelDelete)
>Input Field Input(NullEvent,MouseDown,MouseUp,LineMenu, CircleMenu,RectMenu,DelMenu)
>Field Action(DrawLine,DrawRect,DrawCircle,SaveMousePoint, DelLine,DelRect,DelCircle)

Each field must contain two or more conditions. A two- condition field would be equivalent to an ERL flag with one condition matching the raised and the other the unraised of the flag. ERL has no mechanism for referencing the unraised state of a flag. Condition names must be unique across the PPS. Note that interface status information (ActiveCmnd, DragMode, and Action), inputs (Input), semantic conditions (SelectedObj), and query fields (ConfirmDel) are all uniformly represented as fields in the state space. The only difference between these types of fields is the way in which their condition settings are obtained. The conditions in a field are defined to be mutually exclusive. For example, NoCmnd and LineCmnd cannot be asserted at the same time.

Rules in this state space transform one state into another. Figure 6:10 shows a set of rules that might be used in the drawing application. A rule consists of a left-hand side, or criteria, and a right-hand side, or consequence. The left-hand side is a list of conditions that must be present in the current state and the right-hand side is a list of conditions that will be asserted in the next state.

Fig. 6:10

Partial Rule Set for Drawing Application

>1. NoCmnd, LineMenu -> LineCmnd, NotDragging
>2. NoCmnd, CircleMenu -> CircleCmnd, NotDragging
>3. NoCmnd, RectMenu -> RectCmnd, NotDragging
>4. LineCmnd, MouseDown -> RubberLine, SaveMousePoint
>5. RubberLine, NullEvent -> RubberLine
>6. RubberLine,MouseUp -> NotDragging, DrawLine
>7. DelMenu,LineSel,OKDelete -> DelLine, NoCmnd
>8. DelMenu,RectSel,OKDelete -> DelRect, NoCmnd
>9. DelMenu,CircleSel,OKDelete -> DelCircle, NoCmnd

The rules in figure 6:10 are not sufficient to implement the example application but they are sufficient to illustrate the points that follow. It is also important to note that the rules are arranged in lowest to highest order of priority. When two rules are in conflict, as will be discussed later, the higher priority rule takes precedence.

The expressive power of a PPS (and ERL) is derived from the fact that a single rule may actually apply to a multitude of states. For example, consider the condition list: (LineCmnd, MouseDown). This condition list, if used as the left-hand side of a rule, would match 280 different states including:

> (**LineCmnd**,NoSelection, NotDragging,OKDelete,**MouseDown**,
> DrawLine)
>
> or
>
> (**LineCmnd**,CircleSel, NotDragging, OKDelete,**MouseDown**,
> DrawCircle)

It is this ability to define behavior on a large number of states that gives production systems a significant expressive advantage over the other event-handling models.

Semantic Actions

Simply transforming states does not accomplish much. We must attach semantic actions to the PPS so that it will do something. Semantic actions are attached to conditions. When a condition is asserted the corresponding action will be performed. Some fields, such as Action, are created purely for defining semantic behavior. Others, such as DragMode, define semantic behavior as well as exerting control over the dialog. By arranging semantic actions in mutually exclusive fields we can reason about which actions might conflict with each other and which would not. It is assumed that actions attached to conditions that belong to different fields are independent of each other and will not conflict. This notion of action conflict is important to the inheritance capability of a PPS. Since the variety of forms for semantic actions has already been discussed, only descriptive strings will be used here for exposition purposes.

Examples of condition actions for the drawing application might be:

> NoCmnd: "Remove all menu highlights"
> LineCmnd: "Highlight line menu item"
> NotDragging: "Terminate any drag echoes"
> DrawLine: "Draw a line from the saved"
>   point to the current point"

SaveMousePoint: "Save the current mouse
    location"
DelLine: "Delete the selected line"

Note that in the example rule set, the behavior of ActiveCmnd is partially independent of the DragMode. Using condition actions, each field can be viewed as an independent process that takes care of itself. By combining conditions from various fields in the rules, more refined, interrelated actions can be created. Providing such flexibility in a state machine diagram would lead to a rat's nest of state transition arcs.

Input Processes

It is assumed that the PPS is executed once for each new input. Whatever system is using the PPS would set the input conditions according to the inputs received and would then evaluate the PPS. One facility required of the dialog handler is the ability to enable and disable logical devices. In the example PPS only rules 7, 8, and 9 (see figure 6:10) contain the DelMenu input condition. If, however, the SelectedObj field has the NoSelection condition none of these rules can fire. In such a case DelMenu should be disabled. Each input field must have a semantic Enable/Disable action associated with it which can be called for each condition of the field that is not acceptable as input. The use of these Enable/Disable actions will be discussed in the section on PPS evaluation.

Semantic and Query Fields

Semantic fields (such as SelectedObj) are set by the application code. Their initial conditions are set before starting the PPS. Routines are provided that allow the application to set these conditions at any time. Other than the fact that a semantic field cannot appear on the right-hand side, or consequence, of a rule, such fields are treated just like any other field. The semantic and query fields fill the same function as transition guards when other fields are present in a rule. If only semantic or query fields are present in a rule, then semantic fields function in a similar fashion to a conditional transition. In SASSAFRAS the role of a semantic field would be filled by an event generated by an application module which would then be received by the relevant ERL module and used to set a local flag.

Query fields are also set by the application, but only on demand. Each query field has an associated query action which is executed whenever the field's condition is needed by a rule. The special nature of query fields is that if there are no rules that can fire which are dependent on the value of that field, then the field's condition is never requested. In the example PPS we would not want to ask for the condition of ConfirmDel unless we were actually trying to execute a delete. If DelMenu is the condition of Input and LineSel is the condition of SelectedObj then rule 7 could fire. At this point a value must be obtained for the ConfirmDel field in order to determine if rule 7 should fire. There is, however, no rule that contains both the MouseDown and either of the conditions of ConfirmDel. If MouseDown is the condition of Input then the query action for ConfirmDel need not be executed since no rule depends on the result.

Providing the query mechanism in ERL would require two events to be sent. A dialog-handling ERL module would need to send a message requesting the query and whatever module handled the query would have to send a return message.

Inheritance

The major goal of having one PPS inherit behavior from another PPS is to be able to reuse portions of that behavior without needing to understand it completely. PPS inheritance is additive in that it allows the existing fields and rules of the inherited PPS to be reused without change and allows new fields to be defined and new rules to be added. The one restriction is that none of the inherited conditions may appear on the right-hand side of a new rule. Using inherited conditions in tests, or left-hand sides, allows the inherited rules to interact with the new rules. Forbidding inherited conditions from appearing in the consequence of a new rule prevents the new rules from interfering with the actions of the inherited PPS.

Take as an example the PPS previously described and assume that we want to extend this system to show the dimensions of an object whenever it is selected, as in figure 6:11.

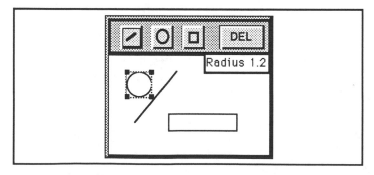

Fig. 6:11
Extended
Drawing
Application

We would inherit the previously defined fields and rules and add the following new fields:

```
Field DimDraw(
    LineLength: "Draw the length of the selected line",
    CircleRad: "Draw the radius of the selected circle",
    RectDim: "Draw the dimensions of the selected rectangle")
Field Redraw( NoDimDraw, DimRedraw)
```

and the following rules:

A1. LineMenu -> DimRedraw
A2. CircleMenu->DimRedraw
A3. RectMenu -> DimRedraw
A4. DelMenu -> DimRedraw
A5. MouseDown -> DimRedraw
A6. LineSel, DimReDraw -> LineLength,NoDimDraw
A7. CircleSel, DimReDraw -> CircleRad, NoDimDraw
A8. RectSel,DimReDraw -> RectDim,NoDimDraw

The inherited rules (1-9 in figure 6:10) always have a lower priority than the new rules (A1-A8 shown above). Note that the old functionality will not be changed since the condition actions of DimDraw will not affect the other field actions in any way. The inherited rules will still fire under the same circumstances since they cannot conflict with the new rules. The Redraw field is used to make sure that the drawing of the dimensions only happens once.

Rules and fields can be inherited from more than one PPS. The only modification that must be made is to condition and field names to prevent multiple conditions with the same name. With this inheritance model, existing functionality can be reused and expanded as needed. The new fields can provide additional actions and state information without interfering with the inherited fields and rules. Such an inheritance facility is possible because of the inherent parallelism in the multiple fields.

Formal Definitions

There are a number of definitions that are required before proceeding with the PPS evaluation algorithm. These definitions are best illustrated by the following simple PPS state space definition.

```
Field X(A,B,C)
Field Y( P,Q)
Field Z( T,U,V)
```

Condition Vectors and State Sets

The primary expressive vehicle in a PPS is the condition vector. A condition vector consists of a list of conditions where no pair of conditions are members of the same field. Not every field needs to be represented in the vector. Those fields for which no condition is specified are marked as don't cares.

A condition vector represents a set of states from the state space. For example, the condition vector

     (A,T)

represents the following set of states.

     { (A,P,T), (A,Q,T) }

Treating a condition vector as a set of states, we can define several set operations on condition vectors.

Subset

CVa is a subset of CVb iff every condition appearing in CVb also appears in CVa. For example:

     (B,T) is a subset of (B)
        because (B,T) = { (B,P,T), (B,Q,T) }
        both of which are members of (B)

     (B,T) is not a subset of (B,Q)
        because (B,T) contains (B,P,T)
        which is not a member of (B,Q)

Intersection

CVr equals CVa intersect CVb iff every condition in CVa appears in CVr as well as every condition in CVb, and CVr does not have more than one condition for any field. For example:

     (B,T) intersect (Q,T) = (B,Q,T)
     (B,T) intersect (Q,U) = empty because
        (B,T) cannot contain any state with the condition U.

Overlay

     CVr = (CVa overlay CVb) iff
        For each field F
            If CVa.F is a don't care then
                CVr.F =CVb.F
            Else
                CVr.F = CVa.F

The overlay result (CVr) can be described as CVb with sufficient fields changed to match CVa. This is the basic operation used when applying the consequence of a rule. For example,

$$(A,P) \text{ overlay } (Q,T) = (A,P,T)$$
$$(A) \text{ overlay } (B,P,U) = (A,P,U)$$
$$(Q) \text{ overlay } (B) = (B,Q)$$

Partial Independence

A condition vector CVa is partially independent of CVb iff there is at least one field that has a condition in CVa that does not have a condition in CVb. The notion of partial independence is important in deciding if a rule's consequence has something new to assert which does not conflict with what is already known.

CVa is partially independent of CVb iff
  CVa intersects CVb
    and
  CVb is not a subset of CVa

For example,

(B,V) is partially independent of (B)
  (B,V) is a subset of (B) (which can also contain (B,U))
(B,V) is partially independent of (P)
B,V) is not partially independent of (B,P,V)
  all conditions in (B,V) have already been
  asserted by (B,P,V)

Evaluation of a PPS

Having defined a PPS, as well as a number of operations on condition vectors, it is now possible to describe the evaluation of a PPS. At run time we can create instances of a PPS and associate an instance with a window. Each instance contains a pointer to the PPS definition and a current state (CS). In order to resolve conflicts at run time we augment the current state with a condition vector (KC) to represent the known conditions. Each time we obtain an input from the event queue, we set the appropriate input fields of the current state as dictated by our logical event structure, we set KC to contain only the input conditions, and we evaluate the PPS. The algorithm is shown in figure 6:12.

Fig. 6:12
Fig. 6:12
PPS Evaluation Algorithm for a Single Input Event

    CS = *whatever value resulted from the application of this algorithm to*
        the previous input.
    GetEvent(E);
    KC = *The input conditions as dictated by E. All other*
        fields are don't cares.
    CS = KC overlay CS
    For each rule R in highest to lowest order
      {If CS is a subset of R.lhs and
          R.rhs is partially independent of KC then
      {KC = KC overlay R.rhs
      Perform the semantic actions associated with the conditions in
      R.rhs.
      }
    }
    CS = KC overlay CS.

The use of KC prevents any condition from being changed more than once. KC is only initialized to the input conditions so that any conditions in the current state, other than the inputs, can be changed at least once. By working in highest to lowest order any conflicts are resolved because KC blocks any lower priority rule from changing conditions asserted by higher priority rules. KC also accumulates the new field settings dictated by the triggered rules, without changing CS. Not changing CS until the end is very important in preventing race conditions in the machine.

Input Field Enable/Disable

We are concerned with interactive behaviors rather than general event handling, and so it is important to enable and disable input fields. Before accepting any inputs we check the current state (CS) of the machine and the rule set to determine which inputs might be acceptable. We first create the known state (KS), which is all fields from CS with any input or query fields marked as don't cares (since we will not know what the conditions of either of these kinds of fields will be after all of the inputs have been received). The algorithm for input enabling is shown in figure 6:13.

CS = *whatever value resulted from the application of this algorithm to the previous input.*

KS = CS with all input and query fields marked as don't cares.

Disable all input conditions

For each rule R
  {INT = KS intersect R.lhs
  If INT is not empty then
    For each input field F
      {**If INT.F is not a don't care then**
        {**Enable INT.F**}
      }
  }

GetEvent(E);

KC = *The input conditions as dictated by E. All other fields are don't cares.*

CS = KC overlay CS

For each rule R in highest to lowest order
  {If CS is a subset of R.lhs and
          R.rhs is partially independent of KC then
    {KC = KC overlay R.rhs
    Perform the semantic actions associated with the conditions in
      R.rhs.
    }
  }

CS = KC overlay CS.

Any input condition that is not explicitly enabled by this method, is disabled. Any rule R that cannot possibly be fired, given the current value of CS, has an empty intersection between KS and R.lhs. Of the rules that can be fired, we enable any input condition that is explicitly mentioned.

As an example, suppose that the current state, before inputs are received, is:

(NoCmnd, NoSelection, NotDragging, -?-, -?-, DrawCircle).

Only rules 1, 2, and 3 (see figure 6:10) have nonempty intersections with the current state. These three rules cause LineMenu, CircleMenu, and RectMenu to be enabled. The inputs MouseDown, NullEvent, MouseUp, and DelMenu are left disabled. If, however, the SelectedObj field was set to

LineSel, then the DelMenu input would also be enabled because rule 7 would have a nonempty intersection with the current state.

Query Field Evaluation

The evaluation of query fields is performed while processing each rule of the PPS. Each query field in CS is initially marked as a don't care since its condition is unknown. As each rule is checked to see if it should fire, the rule is also checked to see if it depends on a query field. If such a dependency exists then the query is evaluated and marked as known. The modified algorithm is shown in figure 6:14.

Fig. 6:14

PPS Evaluation Algorithm with Semantic Queries

CS = *whatever value resulted from the application of this algorithm to the previous input.*

KS = *CS with all input and query fields marked as don't cares.*

Disable all input conditions

For each rule R

  {INT = KS intersect R.lhs

  If INT is not empty then

    For each input field F

      {If INT.F is not a don't care then

        {Enable INT.F}

      }

  }

GetEvent(E);

KC = *The input conditions as dictated by E. All other fields are don't cares.*

CS = KC overlay CS

mark all query fields in CS as don't cares

For each rule R in highest to lowest order

  {INT = CS intersect R.lhs

  If INT is not empty and

    R.rhs is partially independent of KC then

    {For each query field Q which has a condition in INT

    {KC.Q=CS.Q = evaluation of Q.Action }

  If CS is a subset of R.lhs then

    {KC = KC overlay R.rhs

    Perform the semantic actions associated with the conditions in R.rhs.

```
            }
          }
        }
      CS = KC overlay CS.
```

As an example, suppose that SelectedObj has the condition LineSel and the input received is DelMenu. As the rules are being evaluated, rule 7 will intersect the current state but the field ConfirmDel will be unknown. The intersection of the current state with rule 7's left-hand side would contain OKDelete, which is a condition of the unknown field ConfirmDel. ConfirmDel would be evaluated (which might consist of asking the user if deletion was OK). After evaluation ConfirmDel is now known and rule 7 may or may not fire depending on the result. Note that if the input had not been DelMenu, rules 7 to 9 would not intersect the current state and, therefore, would never cause ConfirmDel's action to be evaluated.

PPS Implementation

A drawback to using production systems is the cost of testing each production for a match. In the case of both ERL and PPS this can be reduced by using a bit vector representation of the condition lists. An advantage that a PPS has over ERL is that the bit vectors are more compact and can accommodate a larger state space within a 32-bit word.

In a PPS each field is given a sufficient number of bits to encode all of its conditions. For example, a field with 4 conditions is allocated 2 bits, while a field with 5 conditions is allocated 3 bits. Within those bits each condition is given a unique number. Every condition is represented by a value word and every field is represented by a mask word, which has ones in that field's bits and zeros everywhere else. Suppose, for example, that of an 8-bit vector the field ActiveCmnd is allocated bits 0 and 1, SelectedObj is allocated bits 2 and 3, and DragMode is allocated bits 4-6. The encoding is shown in figure 6:15.

Fig. 6:15

Bit Vector Encoding of Fields and Conditions

ActiveCmnd Mask	0 000 00 11
NoCmnd	0 000 00 00
LineCmnd	0 000 00 01
CircleCmnd	0 000 00 10
RectCmnd	0 000 00 11

SelectedObj Mask	0 000 11 00
NoSelection	0 000 00 00
LineSel	0 000 01 00
CircleSel	0 000 10 00
RectSel	0 000 11 00
DragMode Mask	0 111 00 00
RubberLine	0 000 00 00
RubberCircle	0 001 00 00
RubberRect	0 010 00 00
DragSelect	0 011 00 00
NotDragging	0 100 00 00

A condition is then uniquely defined by its value and its mask. A condition list is also represented by a value word and a mask word. A condition list is formed by ORing the masks and values of its component conditions to produce a new mask and value for the condition list. The following are examples of such condition lists.

	Value	Mask
(RectCmnd, LineSel)	0 000 01 11	0 000 11 11
(CircleSel, RubberRect)	0 010 10 00	0 111 11 00

The purpose of the mask words is to encode the don't cares as zeros. We can define each of the condition vector operations in terms of such bit vectors.

A is a subset of B iff   (A.mask AND B.mask) == B.mask
and
(B.value == (A.value AND B.mask))

A intersect B == R
  Overlap = A.mask AND B.mask
  If (A.value AND Overlap) == (B.value AND Overlap) then
    R.mask = A.mask OR B.mask
    R.value = A.value OR B.value
  Else
    R=empty;

A overlay B == R
  R.mask = A.mask OR B.mask
  R.value = (B.value AND (NOT A.mask)) OR A.value

The bit vector definitions of condition lists can be encoded within 32 to 64 bits in most cases. This encoding means that testing a rule for firing, and

---

actually executing the firing, will only take a very few AND and OR instructions, which are very fast on most machines.

Optimizations

Two major optimizations have been defined which improve the run-time performance of a PPS.

Rule Elimination

Removing rules from a PPS obviously reduces the cost of testing rules to see if they can fire. There are two cases in which a rule can be eliminated from a PPS.

Removing Rules that cannot Fire

If

> 1. R1 has lower priority than R2 and
> 2. R1.lhs is a subset of R2.lhs and
> 3. R1.rhs is not partially independent of R2.rhs

Then

> R1 can be eliminated because it will never fire.

If the first two tests are true, then whenever R1 might fire, R2 will have already fired. If test three is true then R1 will conflict with R2 and will never fire.

Removing Rules that are Redundant

If

> 1. R1 has **higher** priority than R2 and
> 2. R1.lhs is a subset of R2.lhs and
> 3. R1.rhs is a subset of R2.rhs and
> 4. There is no rule R3 between R1 and R2
>   such that R3.lhs intersects R1.lhs

Then

> R1 can be eliminated because all of its function is subsumed by R2.

If tests 1 and 2 succeed then in all cases where R1 might fire it is also possible for R2 to fire. If test 3 succeeds then anything that R2 might do will be done by R1 anyway. If there is a rule (R3) that lies between R1 and R2, but which conflicts with R1 and R2, then R1 must be retained. Otherwise, if R1 was removed then R3's action (in the conflict cases) would no longer be overridden by R1. This is the purpose of test 4.

Rule Indexing

Indexing the rule list based on one or more fields provides another optimization. Indexing partitions the rule list according to the conditions of the indexed field, or fields. Rules with don't cares for the indexed fields will appear in multiple partitions. Rule indexing on the input field and state field, for example, would produce the normal two- dimensional state transition table.

Partitioning the rule list serves to reduce the number of rules that must be matched for each cycle through the machine. An unindexed PPS executes in a time proportional to the number of rules. An indexed PPS (given a good indexing choice) can reach, or closely approach constant time execution in most cases. As an example figure 6:16 shows the original example rule set after it has been indexed on the Input field.

Fig. 6:16

Rule List Indexed on Input

> NullEvent:
>   5) RubberLine, NullEvent -> RubberLine
> MouseDown:
>   4) LineCmnd, MouseDown ->
>   RubberLine, SaveMousePoint
> MouseUp:
>   6) RubberLine,MouseUp -> NotDragging, DrawLine
> LineMenu:
>   1) NoCmnd, LineMenu -> LineCmnd, NotDragging
> CircleMenu:
>   2) NoCmnd, CircleMenu -> CircleCmnd, NotDragging
> RectMenu:
>   3) NoCmnd, RectMenu -> RectCmnd, NotDragging
> DelMenu:
>   7) DelMenu,LineSel,OKDelete -> DelLine, NoCmnd
>   8) DelMenu,RectSel,OKDelete -> DelRect, NoCmnd
>   9) DelMenu,CircleSel,OKDelete -> DelCircle, NoCmnd

Note that in the indexed version of the rule list only DelMenu has more than one rule to check. The DelMenu rule list could be further indexed on the SelectedObj field to produce a unique mapping.

Not all choices of indexing fields are good. Figure 6:17 shows the example rule list indexed on the ActiveCmnd field.

NoCmnd:

    1) NoCmnd, LineMenu -> LineCmnd, NotDragging

    2) NoCmnd, CircleMenu -> CircleCmnd, NotDragging

    3) NoCmnd, RectMenu -> RectCmnd, NotDragging

    5) RubberLine, NullEvent -> RubberLine

    6) RubberLine,MouseUp -> NotDragging, DrawLine

    7) DelMenu,LineSel,OKDelete -> DelLine, NoCmnd

    8) DelMenu,RectSel,OKDelete -> DelRect, NoCmnd

    9) DelMenu,CircleSel,OKDelete -> DelCircle,NoCmnd

LineCmnd:

    4) LineCmnd, MouseDown ->

         RubberLine, SaveMousePoint

    5) RubberLine, NullEvent -> RubberLine

    6) RubberLine,MouseUp -> NotDragging, DrawLine

    7) DelMenu,LineSel,OKDelete -> DelLine, NoCmnd

    8) DelMenu,RectSel,OKDelete -> DelRect, NoCmnd

    9) DelMenu,CircleSel,OKDelete -> DelCircle,NoCmnd

CircleCmnd:

    5) RubberLine, NullEvent -> RubberLine

    6) RubberLine,MouseUp -> NotDragging, DrawLine

    7) DelMenu,LineSel,OKDelete -> DelLine, NoCmnd

    8) DelMenu,RectSel,OKDelete -> DelRect, NoCmnd

    9) DelMenu,CircleSel,OKDelete -> DelCircle,NoCmnd

RectCmnd:

    5) RubberLine, NullEvent -> RubberLine

    6) RubberLine,MouseUp -> NotDragging, DrawLine

    7) DelMenu,LineSel,OKDelete -> DelLine, NoCmnd

    8) DelMenu,RectSel,OKDelete -> DelRect, NoCmnd

    9) DelMenu,CircleSel,OKDelete -> DelCircle,NoCmnd

Since the ActiveCmnd field is a don't care in rules 5-9 these rules are part of every sublist. In practice, the rules are not duplicated. However, the number of rules that must be checked is not significantly improved by indexing on ActiveCmnd. Figure 6:17 shows that indexing can also consume additional space. Algorithms have been defined which, given a maximum size, will automatically select an indexing scheme that fits the PPS machine within that space, while attempting to minimize the size of the largest rule list partition.

Production Systems and other Event Handling Models

The production system model is formally equivalent to finite state machines and regular languages. Its expressive model (the way in which the machine is specified) is a direct superset of a variety of other UIMS models.

State Machines

A state machine is easily represented in ERL with a flag for each state and a rule for each transition. Each rule raises the flag of the next state as well as performing the transition action.

A state machine is simply a PPS which has:

1. a state field with conditions for all of the states,
2. an input field with conditions for all of the logical inputs,
3. an action field with conditions for all of the semantic actions.

Each rule has a state and an input on the left-hand side with the action and next state on the right-hand side.

Event Dispatchers

The window event-handling systems are represented in ERL by omitting any flags. Input events are translated directly into semantic application events. In an equivalent PPS there would only be an input field and an action field with one rule for each input condition. The rule would simply translate the input condition into an action condition.

Summary

Production systems dialog models enhance the state machine models by providing parallelism and communication between machines. Such production systems also enhance the event handlers by providing syntactic dialog control and a uniform mechanism for semantic dialog control. In ERL syntactic control is provided by flags. In PPS the conditions within fields provide syntactic control. A PPS implementation also has an inheritance capability which allows user interfaces to be readily extended without interfering with existing functionality. The bit vector implementation and the optimizations shown for a PPS remove any loss of efficiency incurred by adopting a production system model.

Production systems are primarily for use by dialog authors. The primary concern of this model is the sequencing of inputs. Architecturally, the rules of a production system would be part of the dialog specification and would be used to drive the dialog manager. There is no model for acquiring and releasing devices, but the enable and disable functions have been developed.

References

1 Hill, R.D. *Supporting Concurrency, Communication, and Synchronization in Human-Computer Interaction — The Sassafras UIMS.* **ACM Transactions on Graphics** 5(3): 179-210, July 1986.

2 Olsen, D.R. *Propositional Production Systems for Dialog Description.* **Human Factors in Computing Systems (CHI '90),** April 1990, 57-63.

7.
Dialog Trees

All of the dialog models discussed so far have been concerned with the handling of interactive inputs. The overall structure of the dialog was left to the dialog authors. Each dialog model introduces biases into the dialog design process, but the exact syntax of the dialog is left to the designers.

This chapter will introduce dialog trees. Dialog trees were the first UIMS model that considered the overall structure of a class of dialogs and designed a tool to fit that structure specifically. Dialog trees are also interesting because they form the basis of the Tiger[1] UIMS which has one of the longest histories of actual application. Tiger and its successor products have been used in practice for a number of years by Boeing Computer Services and, more recently, by Electronic Data Systems and General Motors.

Tiger was primarily designed for CAD applications in the aircraft industry. Such highly specialized programs have a very large number of commands, options, and variants on commands. A major user interface design problem is to organize and present such complexity to a user in a fashion that can be easily navigated and understood. A second characteristic of this environment is that users must frequently work with a variety of programs, each with its own user interface. A consistent user interface strategy is imperative to maximize the cross-training between applications.

The overall philosophy of dialog trees consists of selecting from a very large set of semantic actions and then collecting arguments for those actions before invoking them. The difference compared with other dialog models is one of point of view. Rather than building the dialog around event handling, the dialog is built around a model of what the user is trying to accomplish. In the dialog tree model the belief is that a user is trying to select some action and to associate arguments with that action.

The dialog tree model presented in this chapter does not represent the full implementation of Tiger. The algorithms presented here are designed for clear exposition rather than an explicit reconstruction of Kasik's approach.

Basic Algorithm

The primary structure for dialog trees is, of course, a tree (see *figure 7:1*).

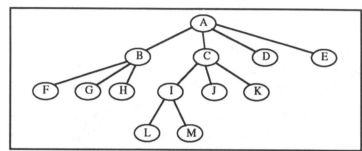

Fig. 7:1
*Example
Dialog Tree*

The leaves of the tree are the individual commands a user can invoke. The state of the dialog consists of the current node of the tree on which the user is working. In this discussion the nodes are simply given letters. In actual applications each node has an associated prompt string which represents the meaning of selecting that node. All subnodes of the current node are available for selection. For example, if node C in figure 7:1 is the current node, then nodes I, J, and K are available for selection. If we associate a logical event device with each node selection, then we must acquire and enable each of the logical devices associated with the subnodes of the current node.

In addition to a logical device and a set of subnodes, each node of the tree has a movement specification that must be taken after selecting that node. This movement specification is a nonnegative integer indicating the number of levels to move up the tree. Figure 7:2 shows the tree modified to include these movement specifications.

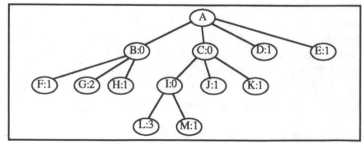

Fig. 7:2
*Dialog Tree with
Movement
Specifications*

If one is at node C, the items I, J, and K are visible. If J is selected then the user would be at node C again, which is one above J. If I is selected then I will become the current node since the movement on I is zero levels.

Enter/Exit Actions

Each node can have an Enter action which is performed whenever that node is selected. A node can also have an Exit action associated with it, which is performed whenever exiting the node. Given the tree in figure 7:2 and a current node of A, a user might then select B which would execute B's Enter action and make B the current node, since the movement number is zero. The selectable nodes are then F, G, and H. If H is selected by the user then both the Enter and Exit actions of H (if it has both) are executed and the current node remains B which is one higher than H. If G is selected then A becomes the current node due to G's movement specification of 2. By selecting G and then moving to A, the Enter and Exit actions of G are executed followed by the Exit action of B.

Arguments and Command Execution

The discussion so far has only provided for the selection of nodes and the execution of entry and exit routines. For a node to invoke an actual semantic command, an Enable and an Execute action must be attached to the node. When such a node is entered its Enable action is executed after its Enter action. While in an Enable action, Tiger provides a number of routines that can be invoked and global variables that can be set while in an Enable action. Calling such routines and setting global variables will describe to Tiger the kinds of arguments that this command wants. For example, if a command were to draw a curve by indicating a list of points with a tablet, then the body of the Enable routine might appear as follows.

```
EnableCurve
{ EnableTabletPoints();
MinimumPoints=2;
MaximumPoints=40;
Prompt="Enter Points for a Curve";
}
```

After the Enable action has been performed, Tiger begins accepting argument inputs from the user according to the setup defined in the Enable action. There are a number of interactive techniques and settings that have been included in Tiger. And the full extent of what can be specified in an Enable action will not be discussed here. After the interactive user has entered the required inputs, the arguments are assembled into a data structure which is then passed to the Execute action, which actually performs the semantic operations. The nature of the data in the argument structure is determined by the interactive technique selected in the Enable action.

Given the preceding discussion the algorithm for the simple dialog handler is as follows.

```
CurrentNode= RootNode;
AcquireAllSubNodes(CurrentNode);
Repeat
  EnableAllSubNodes(CurrentNode);
  GetEvent(Evnt);
  SN=SelectSubNode(CurrentNode,Evnt);
  if SN.Enter exists then
    Perform SN.Enter
  if SN.Enable exists then
    { Perform SN.Enable
    Accept arguments according to current enable
      settings
    Perform SN.Execute(theArguments);
    }
  Count=SN.Movement;
  While Count > 0 do
    { if SN.Exit exists then
        Perform SN.Exit;
      SN=SN.ParentNode;
      Count=Count-1;
    }
  if CurrentNode<>SN then
    { ReleaseAllSubNodes(CurrentNode);
    AcquireAllSubNodes(SN);
    CurrentNode=SN:
    }
Until Quit
```

Layered Menus and Defaults

Tiger was built to handle applications characterized by a large number of commands and options. In such a domain navigating a large dialog tree is a serious problem. Not only can the user become lost in the tree or not know where to find a particular command, but also traversing the tree may require many inputs. Given the example tree in figure 7:2 and a current node of I, a user wanting to invoke command F would have to input L, B, and then F. In a small tree this is not too bad, but if the tree contains 200 nodes it may require 5-7 inputs to get to the desired command. This problem is further complicated if the user needs to switch back and forth frequently between command I and F in order to accomplish some task. Admittedly, an appropriate organization of the tree might relieve such long-distance switching but dialog designers cannot predict all possible working situations that might arise.

The Tiger solution to these problems is to use defaults and a multilayered menu. By presenting many layers of the dialog tree in the menu, rather than just one, the user has a wider visible scope of action and a better global view of the interaction. By using the last selection and arguments entered at a given node as the defaults, returning to a previous state is greatly facilitated.

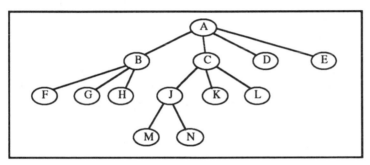

Fig. 7:3

Given the dialog tree in figure 7:3, let M be the current selected node. The menus for all levels of the tree from M's siblings to the root are presented in a layered fashion as shown below.

      B C D E
      J K L
  >   M N

The underlined entries show the selected item at each level and the pointer shows the level that contains the current node. This presentation of the menu gives the user a clear global picture of the current state of the dialog.

Since all the menu items for all the levels are displayed on the screen they can all be selected. If the user wants to get to command F from M, only B needs to be selected to move up the tree. From there the F item will be visible and can be selected. The selection of B to move up the menu tree

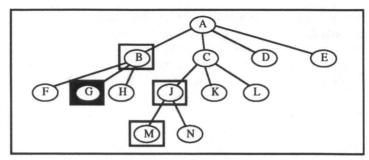

Fig. 7:4

*Dialog Tree
with Default
Selections*

is called an implicit reject of the current selection. By selecting B the Exit actions for M, I, and C are all performed before the Enter action on B. This ability to select any item in the layered menu eliminates the need for the movement numbers to control movement up the tree after selection. If the user wants to move up the tree, the higher level item is selected.

Tiger remembers previously selected nodes as well as any arguments gathered for the commands at those nodes. Figure 7:4 shows the dialog tree augmented to show the previously selected nodes with boxes around them. The current node is G.

Let us suppose that the user wants to go to command M and begin entering arguments. The user selects C, which will perform the implicit reject of items G and B. The menu will now appear as in figure 7:5.

Fig. 7:5

```
>  B C D E
   J K L
   M N
```

Note that the current level marker points to the node with C in it but that the submenu under C, as well as that under J, have also been displayed. The lower menu levels are produced because the previous selections have been tentatively chosen as defaults and displayed as if they had been chosen. The current level marker shows us that they have not actually been entered but only displayed.

In order to demonstrate how these defaults can be used, let us assume that node C does not have an Enable action and does not want any arguments. Assume that node J has enabled a keyboard type-in of a string, and that node M has enabled two points to be entered with the tablet. Given these assumptions and the menu shown in figure 7:5 the following scenarios might occur.

Scenario 1. The user selects node M. In order to reach item M several things must occur. The routine J.Enter must be executed followed by J.Execute (J.Enable was performed when J was displayed). When J.Execute is performed by default the argument string used last time is passed again as a default argument. M.Enter is then executed. M.Enable was previously executed so the user may begin entering the two points that M needs.

Scenario 2. The user starts typing on the keyboard. Since C does not need a string, Tiger moves down the tree to the next default selection which is J. J.Enter is executed. Since J.Enable has indicated that J would like a string, J.Execute will be passed the string when it is complete and J will become the new current node.

Scenario 3. The user enters a point with the tablet. Node C does not need a point so the current node moves to J and J.Enter is executed. Since J does not need a point, J.Execute is called with its default argument (the last string entered for J). The current node then moves to M. M.Enter is executed and since M does want a point the input proceeds until both points have been entered at which time M.Execute is called with those points.

Scenarios 2 and 3 demonstrate how Tiger infers from the inputs the correct node to select and how previously entered arguments can be used as defaults. Complex commands with many variants and settings can be represented as chains of commands in the menu tree. The use of defaults means that standard settings can be retained and reused with minimal user effort. Returning to previous work is simple because of the default navigation. With all of the defaults the user is still free to choose a new path or settings whenever needed.

Reenter

Tiger also provides the idea of nodes that can be reentered. Let us suppose that our application has a calculator in it. We could put the subtree for the calculator under a CALC menu item as a subtree of A. The item CALC would appear in the menu as in figure 7:6.

Fig. 7:6

```
      B C D E CALC
      J K L
    > M N
```

CALC would be marked as a reenter node. If the user then selects CALC the resulting menu would be as in figure 7:7.

```
B C D E CALC
J K L
M N
---- CALC ----
> the menus for CALC
```

When CALC was selected a new subinstance of the dialog tree was created below the current node. The user may now operate in CALC as needed. By selecting M from the menu the user can reject the CALC dialog. The dialog for M that was underway when CALC was selected will remain unaffected. The user can immediately continue as before. The TIGER reenter function was the inspiration for reenter states in state machines.

Semantic Control of the Dialog

As with other dialog models, TIGER needs to allow the application code to have some control over the dialog. This is handled by associating a condition action with a node. If a node has a condition action, it is evaluated before the node's menu item is placed on the screen. If the condition returns false, then the node's menu item is acquired but disabled. This is similar to the guards used in state machines.

Full Dialog Tree Traversal Algorithm

This section will present the actual algorithm for processing dialog trees with defaults and implicit rejects. The reenter facility has been omitted to simplify the presentation. There are three components to this algorithm. The first part is the lexical interface, which has been changed to allow for the leveled menus and input handling. The second is the master event loop which receives and dispatches events. The third part is the creation of the leveled menus from the dialog tree information.

Dialog Tree Structure

A dialog tree consists of nodes. Each node has the following properties which control the user interface:

> DialogNode =
> Parent
> > *A pointer to the node which is the parent of this*
> > *node in the tree.*

Enter
>   *The semantic action to be performed when*
>   *this node is entered.*

Exit
>   *The semantic action to be performed when*
>   *this node is exited*

Execute
>   *The semantic action to be performed when*
>   *the node's arguments have been received.*

Enable
>   *The action invoked to setup the kinds of*
>   *argument inputs that Execute is to receive.*

Condition
>   *This action must return true for this node to be*
>   *enabled. This action provides semantic control*
>   *of the dialog.*

Subnodes
>   *A list of all of the subnodes of this node.*

LastSelectedSubnode
>   *The subnode that was selected the last time that*
>   *this node was used.*

DefaultArg
>   *The argument data that was used the last time that*
>   *Execute was evaluated.*

All of the algorithms in this section are driven by the DialogNode data structure.

Lexical Interface

The lexical interface is still defined in terms of acquiring, enabling, and getting events, but now, when devices are acquired, the dialog handler specifies the menu level for which they are acquired. This menu level applies not only to logical menu definitions but also to other inputs such as tablet or mouse inputs. The purpose for associating levels with nonmenu inputs is that the level also controls the traversal through the dialog tree.

The routines that make up the lexical interface are:

ClearLogicalDevices
>   Clears out all existing device acquisitions so that the menu
>   structure can be rebuilt.

Acquire(D, L)

Acquires the logical device D at level L. In the case of menu items, the level L specifies where the menu item should appear. If the logical device D has already been acquired at a different level, then this new acquisition will be ignored. Ignoring subsequent acquistions of a logical device places a priority on its first acquisition. This priority will be used in the algorithm for handling argument inputs. The logical devices for menu items are all disjoint. When devices are acquired they are disabled.

Enable(D)

Enables the logical device D.

Highlight(M)

Highlights the menu item M to indicate that it is the selected item from a particular menu level.

GetEvent(E)

Gets the next event.

Each event returned by GetEvent will have the normal information. In addition, every event will have a Level field which indicates the tree level at which the corresponding logical device was acquired, and, menu item events will have a SelectedNode field which contains the tree node associated with the menu item.

Main Event Handling

The dialog is driven by the dialog tree and the two variables CurrentLevel and CurrentNode. These two variables keep track of our current location in the dialog.

```
CurrentLevel = 0;
CurrentNode = Root;
Repeat
  { SetupMenu();
  GetEvent(Evnt);
  if (Evnt.Level > CurrentLevel)
    { /* Process default selections down to the selected level */
    while (Evnt.Level > CurrentLevel)
      { Execute CurrentNode.Execute with
            CurrentNode.DefaultArg;
      CurrentNode = CurrentNode.LastSelectedSubnode;
      Execute CurrentNode.Enter;
      CurrentLevel=CurrentLevel+1;
      }
    }
```

```
else if (Evnt.Level < CurrentLevel)
  { /* Process the implicit reject up to the selected level */
  while (Evnt.Level < CurrentLevel)
    { Execute CurrentNode.Exit;
    CurrentNode = CurrentNode.Parent;
    CurrentLevel=CurrentLevel-1;
    }
  }
if (Evnt is a menu item selection )
  { if (Evnt.SelectedNode <> CurrentNode)
    { Execute CurrentNode.Exit
    Execute Evnt.SelectedNode.Enter;
    CurrentNode = Evnt.SelectedNode;
    CurrentNode.Parent.LastSelectedSubnode =
        CurrentNode;
    }
  }
else /* Evnt is an argument input */
  { Add Evnt to the inputs being collected for CurrentNode.
  if (all of the inputs have been received for CurrentNode )
    {Execute CurrentNode.Execute with the collected
        inputs
    CurrentNode.DefaultArg = the collected inputs;
    }
  }
}
```

The algorithm functions by first getting an event and using the associated level to adjust the current node. If the event is higher in the tree then implicit rejects are performed to move up. If the event is lower in the tree then defaults are used for moving down. If the event is a menu selection at the same level then the previous node is exited and the new node entered. Once the correct level is reached and the current node updated, argument events can be handled. Exactly how these events are collected and who signals that all specified arguments are present is very much dependent upon the particular interactive techniques associated with the dialog tree implementation.

Initial Menu Setup

A key part of the algorithm is the setup of the layered menus and the correct acquisition and enabling of the logical inputs. The acquisition of devices at the correct level and the enabling of devices in the correct order controls the main event loop. This algorithm is as follows:

```
SetupMenu()
  { int TmpLevel, TmpNode, TmpCurNode=0, Done = False;
  ClearLogicalDevices();
  for (TmpLevel=1; !Done; ++TmpLevel)
    { if (TmpLevel=CurrentLevel)
      { Mark this menu level as current; }
    For each subnode S of TmpCurNode
      { Acquire(S.Device,TmpLevel);
      if (S.Condition == NULL) Then
        { Enable(S.Device ); }
      else if (S.Condition evaluates to true) then
        { Enable(S.Device); }
      if (S==TmpCurNode.LastSelectedSubNode) Then
        { Highlight(S.Device);
        if (TmpLevel >= CurrentLevel) then
          { Evaluate TmpCurNode.Enable;
          Acquire and enable all of the necessary inputs
            for the enabled techniques. Enable them
            at TmpLevel.
          }
        }
      }
    }
    TmpCurNode = TmpCurNode.LastSelectedSubNode;
    Done = TmpCurNode == empty;
    }
  }
```

This algorithm traverses the tree taking the last selected node at each level. Since argument inputs are enabled in top to bottom order, and the acquire routine will disregard duplicate acquisition of the same logical device, the top most instance of an argument input that is at or below the selected node will be the instance that is acquired. This acquisition policy will mean that the correct level will be returned for such devices, and arguments will be handled correctly. Arguments for tree nodes above the current node are not enabled since they have already been executed.

This approach to setting up the menu is somewhat slow. It rebuilds the entire menu upon every event. In many cases, such as selections below the current node, only the highlighting needs to be changed since the displayed items are the same. Such optimizations are possible and even necessary on slower workstations.

Summary

Dialog trees, as embodied in TIGER and its successor products, were the first UIMSs to attempt an holistic view of the dialog management problem. A style of dialog had been created which suited the kinds of user interfaces needed for a broad class of applications. The dialog style is built into TIGERs dialog-handling algorithms so that conforming to the style is a natural and automatic part of the interface development process. Adopting such a style also allows the UIMS to provide a higher level of support than would otherwise be possible.

This model is primarily targeted towards the dialog author. However, portions of the application analyst task and graphics designer task are also involved. The structure of the menu tree and the arguments to be provided for the various semantic commands are very much a part of this model. As such, the application analyst is involved. One of the problems, however, is that the notion is not very friendly to a nonprogrammer. The structure of the menu tree also has a great deal to do with the visual presentation of the dialog which is within the role of the graphics designer. Again the programmer-oriented notation is a problem for this role.

Relative to the UIMS architecture, dialog trees start to combine the semantic interface with the dialog specification and portions of the presentation description. The dialog manager is the primary component that would use this model, although the application code must now be aware of the the the enter, exit, and enable activities in ways that were needed in the other models but were not as formalized. The acquisition and release of logical devices has been modified to include the concept of levels and is automatically derived from the structure of the dialog tree. The enabling and disabling of inputs is handled by the application in setting variables while in the Enable action and also by the conditions that can be placed on tree nodes.

References

1 Kasik, D.J. *A User Interface Management System.* **Computer Graphics** 16(3): 99-106, July 1982.

8.
Language UIMS Models

In the chapter on dialog trees that the emphasis shifted from models for handling inputs towards models that describe the dialog as a whole. In this chapter a family of UIMSs is described that derives its model from the concepts of programming languages. Each of the systems described in this chapter share the following points.

- User interfaces are themselves languages for communicating between users and computers.
- Many user support facilities can be provided by a UIMS if it has a higher level description of what the interface is to accomplish.
- The concepts developed for programming languages can provide a higher level dialog model.

The unifying theme for these systems is that they are driven by a semantic model of the application. This semantic model is defined using the type structure of the underlying programming language. The dialog specification is automatically derived from this semantic model. Most of the interface design work is either in the semantic model or in the presentation.

One of the earliest such systems was EZWin[1] which is based on an object-oriented system built in Lisp. EZWin exploits the dynamic abilities of Lisp in creating and invoking code at run time. The MIKE[2] system is based on Pascal and exploits its type structure as a model for command and menu-based dialogs. Mickey,[3] a descendant of MIKE, generates Macintosh-style interfaces by exploiting additional Pascal type information.

EZWin

EZWin's dialog is modeled after an interactive interpreter built on top of an object-oriented system, which in turn is built in Lisp. The discussion of EZWin presented here has been changed from the original to fit in with the terminology of this book. Readers can refer to the original paper for an "uninterpreted" version. EZWin has three basic kinds of objects: an EZWin object, a Presentation object, and a Command object.

An EZWin object corresponds to the application itself. It consists of a window, a process, the main interaction loop (dialog manager), and some internal state information. Attached to an EZWin object is a list of presentation objects that are to be displayed in the window, a list of command objects, and a list of those commands that are to be permanently displayed on the screen.

A presentation object must be able to handle the following chores:

- drawing itself,
- detecting when it has been selected by the mouse,
- returning the semantic object that it is presenting.

In addition, each presentation object is characterized by its class. The class information is very important in controlling the user interface. The presentation objects are the visual arguments the user is to interact with as part of the interface.

A command object is something that the interface is to do. A command object consists of an advertisement, an argument list definition, and documentation information. The key to EZWin's dialog model is a command object's argument list. Two kinds of arguments can appear in a command's list. The first is the name of a presentation class and the second is the name of an interactive technique class. A command object must also implement a Do-It method which will perform the command when sent the desired arguments.

Building an Example Interface in EZWin

An example will help to illustrate how interfaces are built using EZWin. Let us suppose that we have an application that is to draw boxes with links between them, and to set various attributes of boxes. The semantic definition of such an application might be as follows.

NewBox(Rectangle)	*Create a new box*
NewLink(Box, Box)	*Create a new link between two boxes*
DelBox(Box)	*Delete an existing box*
DelLink(Link)	*Delete an existing link*
MoveBox(Box, Point)	*Move a box to a new location*
Label(Box, String)	*Change the label on a box*
Color(Box, PickColor)	*Change the color of a box*

The interface implementor would create presentation object classes for Box and Link, as well as designing the information required to implement Boxes and Links. The object-oriented nature of EZWin's environment would allow the inheritance of presentation facilities from previously implemented presentation classes such as ShadedRectangle, which could handle many of the interactive chores. Other than this inheritance facility for reuse, the programmer must implement the presentation classes.

In our sample application the implementor must either code or inherit interaction classes for Rectangle, Point, String, and PickColor. In most cases these interaction classes will already be available and need not be reimplemented. The Rectangle class, for example, would provide a rubber-band rectangle facility. The implementor must also create a command object for each command in the semantic definition. A command's advertisement is simply a string to be used for the command when it appears in a menu; the documentation is a string to be displayed when users ask for help; the argument list is a list of classes of arguments that the command needs.

Each of the command objects is placed in the command list of an EZWin object. The commands NewBox and NewLink are placed in the permanent menu list of the EZWin object and any existing Boxes and Links are placed in the EZWin object's presentation list.

When the EZWin object is started, the window would appear as follows.

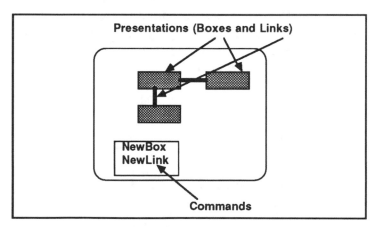

Presentations (Boxes and Links)

NewBox
NewLink

Commands

Fig. 8:1
EZWin

The EZWin object displays the advertisements of all permanent commands in a menu and has each of the presentation objects in the presentation list draw itself.

Sample EZWin Dialogs

The EZWin dialog is driven by the *current command* and the classes of arguments specified so far. EZWin's dialogs consist of selecting commands to be executed and specifying the arguments for the command.

Creating a Box

To create a new box the user could select the NewBox menu item. NewBox would become the current command. Since NewBox (the current command) wants a Rectangle for its argument, the Rectangle interactor is invoked to input a rubber-band rectangle. Once EZWin sees that it has all of the arguments the current command needs, it sends the Do-It message to the NewBox object and passes it the rectangle argument. NewBox can create a new Box argument and add it into the presentation list. The EZWin object notices the new addition and will get it drawn.

Creating a Link

Creating a link will show some of the flexibility of the EZWin dialog model. The user has several options for invoking the link command.

The user could first select the NewLink command from the menu. Once a current command is selected, the other commands in the menu will become mouse insensitive. Since the arguments for NewLink are two Boxes, only the displayed Boxes will be mouse sensitive, the displayed Links will be insensitive. When the user has selected two Boxes from the screen, NewLink will be sent the Do-It message with those two arguments.

The user need not select a command first. Selecting a Box first will cause it to be added to the currently selected arguments. The NewBox menu item will become insensitive because it cannot accept a Box as its first argument. A pop-up menu will be displayed which contains all commands that are not in the permanent menu and will accept a Box as their first argument.

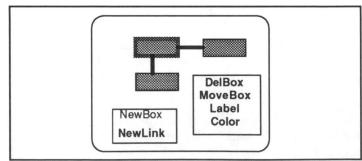

Fig. 8:2
NewLink

Selecting NewLink will cause the pop-up to disappear, since a current command will have been established. Only Boxes will be selectable since the next argument required is a Box. After the second Box is selected the NewLink object is sent the Do-It message and the process starts over again.

After selecting the first Box, the user could have selected a second box. The pop-up would disappear since NewLink is the only command that will accept two boxes as arguments. Selecting NewLink would then establish the current command. Since both arguments for NewLink are already selected the Do-It message is sent immediately.

A Simplified EZWin Dialog Algorithm

The EZWin dialog model is relatively straightforward. The lexical level is handled by the presenter objects, the interactor objects, and the menu items. Each of these can be enabled and disabled. Enabling and disabling a presenter object will control its selectability. Enabling an interactor allows it to take over the interactive events and to return its own logical event. Disabling a menu item will make it unselectable. The pop-up menu only appears when one of its items is enabled. A logical event in this model is a selected or input object.

```
Enable all commands in the Permanent Menu and disable all others;
Enable all presenter objects in the presenter list;
Disable all interactor objects;
CurrentCommand := Null;
ArgStack := Empty;
Repeat
{ If CurrentCommand == Null Then
   { If ArgStack == Empty Then
      {Enable all permanent commands;
       Disable all nonpermanent commands;
       Enable all objects in presenter list;
       Disable all interactor objects;
      }
   Else
      {Disable all presenters;
      For each C in the command list Do
         {If the arguments of C match ArgStack Then
            { If C has an unsatisfied argument Then
                  Enable all presenters whose class is the same
                     as one of C's unsatisfied arguments;
            Enable C;
```

```
              }
            }
          }
        }
      }
    Else CurrentCommand is selected
      { Disable all commands;
      Enable all presenters whose class matches an
        unsatisfied argument of CurrentCommand;
      Enable the interactor whose class matches an
        unsatisfied argument of CurrentCommand;
      }
    GetEvent( E );
    If E is a Presenter or Interactor Then
      { Push E onto ArgStack; }
    Else   { CurrentCommand := E; }
    If CurrentCommand is selected and all arguments satisfied Then
      {Send Do-It to the CurrentCommand
        with ArgStack as arguments;
      CurrentCommand:=Null;
      ArgStack:=Empty;
      }
    }
```

The general approach of the algorithm is to only enable those things that
will lead to a valid combination of command and arguments. When such a
combination is found, it is executed.

MIKE

MIKE (the Menu Interaction Kontrol Environment) was developed in
Pascal, for Pascal programmers. Although many of the same approaches
were used in EZWin, MIKE started out with a very different intent. MIKE
was developed in response to problems that appeared when using
SYNGRAPH and GRINS for actual user interface development. Although
these two tools had sufficient power to build graphical user interfaces
there was a steep learning curve that programmers had to overcome. Most
programmers were reluctant to abandon the familiar concepts of C and
Pascal to program in grammars and state machines.

A second issue addressed by MIKE was the problem of designing a
new interface out of whole cloth. End users and application analysts are
very comfortable in criticizing and requesting improvements to a system

that they can see and use. They are not as good at proposing completely new systems or at evaluating a written user interface specification before it is developed.

The goals for MIKE's development were:

- Provide a higher level UIMS model that would allow many new user interface capabilities to be automatically supported by the UIMS.
- Provide a dialog specification model that would be readily understood by user interface developers and readily explained to nonprogrammers.
- Automatically generate a working interface from a minimal specification and then provide refinement tools for improving the generated interface.
- Integrate the visual layout specification with the dialog and semantic specification.

System Architecture

The MIKE system consists of four major components. These are: the interface editor, the interface profile, the generated semantic interface, and the standard run-time code. All of this is bound together in a Pascal compile and link, as shown in figure 8:3.

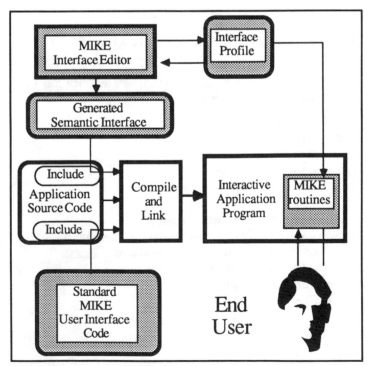

Fig. 8:3

The interface designers work through the *interface editor*, which is a graphical editor written in MIKE. This editor provides access to the *interface profile*, which contains the complete definition of the dialog's semantic and presentation aspects. As with EZWin, MIKE does not have a separate dialog specification. The dialog is controlled by the semantics and the presentation. From the interface profile, the interface editor generates the *semantic interface*. The semantic interface is of the multiparameter command form described in chapter 2. The generated interface is compiled with the application code that implements the application semantics and the standard MIKE run-time routines that manage the dialog. The interface profile is loaded at run time by MIKE's dialog manager to provide the presentation information.

Building an Initial User Interface

Except for its Pascal orientation, MIKE's semantic specification is very similar to EZWin's. The majority of the interface is defined in terms of Pascal data types for the objects to be manipulated by the interactive user, and Pascal procedures for the commands that the user wants to execute.

A simple circuit diagram application is a useful example of how MIKE works. The types of objects manipulated by this application are:

> **Resistor, Capacitor, Wire, Connection**
> *a connection is some point on a resistor, capacitor, or wire component which can be matched with a connection on some other component.*

MIKE only needs to know the names of the types. The application code contains their actual definitions. The commands for this application are:

> **CreateResistor(Ohms:Integer;**
>   **C1:Connection;C2:Connection)**
> **CreateCapacitor(Farads:Integer;**
>   **C1:Connection;C2:Connection)**
> **CreateWire(C1:Connection;C2:Connection)**
>
> **PickConnection(Where: Point):Connection**
> *If Where is over an existing connection, then that connection is returned. Otherwise a new connection is generated at Where*
> **PickResistor(Where: Point):Resistor**
> **PickCapacitor(Where: Point):Capacitor**
> **PickWire(Where: Point):Wire**

```
DeleteResistor( R:Resistor )
DeleteCapacitor( C:Capacitor )
DeleteWire( W:Wire )

MoveResistor( R:Resistor; To:Point)
MoveCapacitor( C:Capacitor; To:Point)
MoveWire( W:Wire; To:Point)

ChangeResistance( Of:Resistor; Ohms:Integer)
ChangeCapacitance( Of:Capacitor; Farads:Integer)

ResistanceOf( R:Resistor):Integer;
CapacitanceOf( C:Capacitor):Integer;

SaveCircuit( FileName:InString )
DiscardCircuit
LoadCircuit( FileName:InString )
```

Note that each command is essentially defined as a Pascal procedure header. Because the specification is almost identical to Pascal, programmers can learn it readily and have a clear understanding of what has to be implemented. By ignoring all of the implementation details, and simply concentrating on the command headers, this specification is easily explained to dialog designers.

In addition to the object types defined for the interface there are a number of types that are predefined and automatically supplied by MIKE. They are:

Integer, Real, Point,

Key,   *A one byte code identifying a function button or keyboard key*

InString   *A character string*

These predefined types identify interactive techniques that are automatically provided by MIKE. They correspond to the interactors in EZWin.

MIKE does not have a textual dialogue specification. All information related to the user interface is defined using MIKE's interface editor. This means that there are no notational forms to be learned. The editor guides the user in specifying command names, arguments, and their types.

Sample MIKE Dialogs

As with EZWin, the dialog is driven by the commands selected and the types of the arguments that are required. One of the decisions that dialog authors must face is the selection of appropriate input techniques for various arguments. MIKE attempts to side step that issue by providing as many input techniques as the current argument type will allow. Commands, for example, are selected either from the menu or by typing enough characters in the command name to uniquely identify them.

MIKE syntax, unlike EZWin, is very command-line oriented. The dialog is a process of selecting commands and specifying arguments. Due to the existence of functions, arguments can also be specified as subexpressions. The general dialog handling algorithm is to present a menu of all of the commands or functions that are consistent with the type of input currently prompted for. The following script represents a dialogue between MIKE and an interactive user for modifying the resistance of some resistor on the screen.

MIKE:	Displays a menu containing

CreateResistor	CreateCapacitor
CreateWire	DeleteResistor
DeleteCapacitor	DeleteWire
MoveResistor	MoveCapacitor
MoveWire	ChangeResistance
ChangeCapacitance	SaveCircuit
DiscardCircuit	LoadCircuit

These are the command procedures that do not return a result.

User: Types "ChangeR"   *unique abbreviation for ChangeResistance*

   or

selects ChangeResistance from the menu

MIKE: Sets the echo and prompt message to
"ChangeResistance (**Of:Resistor __** "
Displays a menu containing
   PickResistor   *The only function that returns a resistor.*

User: Types "P"   *unique abbreviation for PickResistor*

   or

selects PickResistor from the menu

MIKE: Sets the echo and prompt message to
"ChangeResistance (PickResistor (**Where: Point** __"
Clears the menu

User: points to a resistor on the screen using the locator

MIKE: Sets the echo and prompt message to
"ChangeResistance(PickResistor(|Point|),**Ohms:Integer** __"
Displays a menu containing
ResistanceOf   CapacitanceOf
All functions that return integers

User: types in 10000

MIKE: Recognizes that it has a complete command expression
and recursively evaluates the expression by calling
the semantic interface.

The purpose of the command line is to echo to the user what has already been specified and to prompt the user for the kind of argument that should be entered next. EZWin did not have this prompting and echoing, but, on the other hand, EZWin was not limited to only prefix command syntax. In this sample application, the number of functions is limited. The dialog designers could, with little effort, provide a collection of arithmetic and other functions for use in the interface.

Profile Editing

The default dialog shown in the example is not very user friendly. Users must sometimes select commands from a menu of one item; prompts and echoes reek of Pascal syntax; the menu items are in programmerese; and there are no graphical icons. In addition, all of the possible commands appear in a single menu. In a real application with 500 commands this would be untenable. This generated interface does function, however, and does allow users to explore the capabilities of the interface early in the development process.

The interface editor is the mechanism for resolving these difficulties. The interface editor allows dialog authors and graphics designers to tailor the interface with minimum programmer involvement. The editor provides tailoring facilities in three major areas: command selection, prompts/echoes, and visual layout.

Command Selection

The interface editor allows designers to change the names of commands to be more meaningful to users, minimize the length of unique abbreviations, and structure the menu to handle large applications.

The commands in the sample application could have the following renamings.

CreateResistor	=>	New.Resistor
CreateCapacitor	=>	New.Capacitor
CreateWire	=>	New.Wire
DeleteResistor	=>	Remove.Resistor
DeleteCapacitor	=>	Remove.Capacitor
DeleteWire	=>	Remove.Wire
MoveResistor	=>	Move.Resistor
MoveCapacitor	=>	Move.Capacitor
MoveWire	=>	Move.Wire
ChangeResistance	=>	Change.Resistance
ChangeCapacitance	=>	Change.Capacitance
SaveCircuit	=>	Save
DiscardCircuit	=>	Remove.File
LoadCircuit	=>	Load

The dotted notation for names will form the menu into a tree.

New
  Resistor, Capacitor, Wire
Remove
  Resistor, Capacitor, Wire, File
Move
  Resistor, Capacitor, Wire
Change
  Resistance, Capacitance
Save
Load

The interface designers have complete freedom in this structuring without programmer involvement. Since changing the profile does not require a compile step the updates can be performed quickly in response to user requests. In addition to command renaming, accelerator keys can be bound to commands and commands can be hidden so as only to use accelerators. Such hidden accelerators allow commands like ScrollUp to be tied only to the up arrow key and not to appear in the menu.

Echoes and Prompts

The echo is a presentation of a procedure or function and its argument expressions. The default echo can be changed in the interface editor. For example, a default echo of a command in our sample interaction might be

"ChangeResistance(PickResistor(|Point|) , "

This partial expression expects a value for the resistance. Note that |Point| is the default command line echo for point values. A more valuable echo for a point is a marker placed at the screen location actually selected. This form for echoes is accurate but is in a notation that is more suitable for programmers than for end users. The interface designer can modify these echo expressions. The default echo expression for the ChangeResistance command is:

"ChangeResistance(@, @)"

which consists of two parts. The first part, "ChangeResistance," is simply the external name of the command and is changed whenever the external name is changed. The parameter portion of the echo is "(@,@)." The at sign "@" designates where the echo for an argument expression is to be placed. The parameter echo for ChangeResistance can be changed to the expression

" of @ to @ ohms."

The parameter echo of PickResistor can be changed from

"PickResistor(@)"

to an empty string, and its external name to

"SelectedResistor".

Together these will yield a new echo of

"Change.Resistance of SelectedResistor to 75 ohms"

instead of the default

"ChangeResistor(PickResistor(|Point|) , 75)".

The prompt is formed from the name of the current parameter and type of input desired. Both of these names can be changed in the interface editor.

Visual Layout

The visual layout of a MIKE interface is a tree of named viewports as shown in the following diagram.

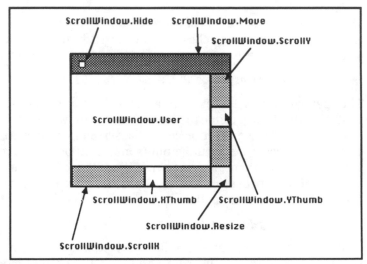

Fig. 8:4
MIKE

These viewports are drawn in the interface editor and can be accessed by name from the application code. In addition, action expressions can be placed on these viewports to invoke command expressions as seen below.

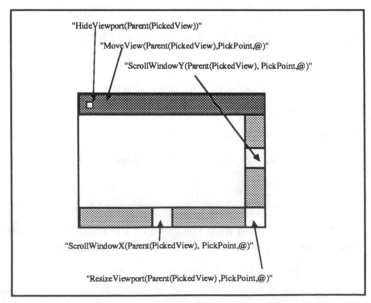

Fig. 8:5

When a viewport is selected, its action expression is inserted into the command line as if it had been entered by the user. The at sign indicates where additional input from the user is required. The use of the at sign is particularly useful in creating iconic menus where all of the arguments are to be supplied by the user.

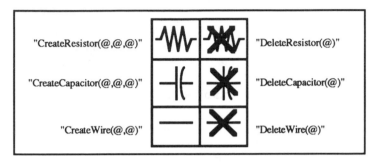

Fig. 8:6

The MIKE visual layout facility is similar to MENULAY, except that the dialog manager of MIKE supports obtaining argument inputs, which event dialogs leave to the application programmer.

MIKE's Dialog Management Algorithm

In addition to handling normal inputs, MIKE supports a rub out and a cancel facility to allow users to back out of erroneous inputs. The dialog management algorithm is a modification of the nondeterministic algorithm for top-down parsing. In this case the backtracking is not part of the parsing process but rather part of the rub out handling.

The algorithm is based on the CMND, TODO, and BACKUP stacks. The CMND stack contains a prefix form of the partially parsed command. The TODO stack contains references to parameters for which arguments have not yet been parsed. The BACKUP stack contains entries from the TODO stack for which arguments have already been placed on to CMND. BACKUP provides the information necessary to perform the rub outs.

```
Quit:=False
While not Quit Do
   {Initialize CMND and BACKUP to empty.
   Place a single dummy parameter with NIL type on the top of TODO.
   While not empty(TODO) and not Quit Do
      {Load the menu list with all commands or functions whose
         result type matches the type of the top entry on TODO.
      Display the menu list in the menu viewport.
      Construct an echo message from the information stored in
         CMND.
```

Add a prompt for the top element on TODO to the echo
message.
Display the echo message in the echo viewport.
GetEvent(E).
If (E is a menu selection) or
   (E is an abbreviation of one of the commands in
      the menu list) Then
   {Pop the top element off of TODO and push it onto BACKUP.
   Push an entry for the selected command onto CMND.
   For every parameter of the selected command push an
      entry onto TODO in reverse order
      (so that they will come off in the correct order).
   }
Else If E is the result of a primitive input technique
        which matches the type of
           the top element on TODO Then
   {Pop the top element off of TODO and push it onto BACKUP
   Push an entry for the result value onto CMND.
   }
Else If I is a Rubout Then
   {If the top element on CMND is a command or function Then
      Pop all of its parameter entries off the top of TODO.
   Pop the top element off of CMND and discard it.
   Pop the top element off of BACKUP and push it back onto TODO.
   }
Else If E is a Cancel Then
   {Initialize BACKUP and CMND to empty.
   Initialize TODO to a single dummy entry with a NIL type.
   }
Else If E is a Quit Then
   {Quit:= True; }
Else
   Report an error and do nothing
   } (* Command Parsing Loop *)
If not Quit Then
   Recursively evaluate the command expression stored in
      CMND by calling the semantic interface.
   } (* Entire interactive program *)

The logical inputs that drive the algorithm given above are not simple button presses, but rather the results of complete interactive techniques. This algorithm must be modified slightly to accommodate menu trees rather than simple command selections. Most of the changes, however, are in the presentation and the lexical handler.

Macros by Example

In addition to the normal presentation editing which the profile editor supports, MIKE also allowed users to extend the interface by defining new commands at run time.[4] To create a new macro command, a user would select a special menu item to start recording the macro. The recording command would ask for the new command's name and the names of any parameters that the command was to have. Since the parameters did not have any type information, their names appeared in all of the menus, enclosed in angle brackets. The user would define the macro by simply invoking the commands that would make up the macro body. These commands would be executed as the user entered them, and the echoes for these commands would appear in the macro window. The macro window would show the user what the constructed macro looked like.

If the user ever wanted to use one of the parameters in the macro they would select the parameter name from the menu. When a parameter is first selected it does not have a type or a sample value to use while demonstrating the macro. The type information is automatically derived from the type of argument that MIKE wants when the parameter is first used. MIKE would then ask the user to provide a sample value for the parameter. After the first reference to the parameter it would in the future only appear in the menu for its type.

One problem with such macro recording facilities is that users frequently make errors while demonstrating the macro. MIKE handles this by allowing the user to step backwards through the macro. Each back step would undo the effect of the command that it stepped across. Such a command, however, is not deleted from the macro unless the user specifically requests such a deletion. Stepping forward through a macro would simply execute the next command in the macro. Users could also point at commands in the macro window and MIKE would either undo back to that command or execute forward to it. This allowed free editing of the macro while in demonstration mode.

When the macro is complete the user turns off recording and the macro definition now consists of a name, a list of parameters, and a body. To the rest of MIKE a macro command appears just like any other command. Users or designers could go into the profile editor to change the echoes, prompts of macros, or associate such macros with icons or other action expressions. The macros are first-class citizens of MIKE's dialog model.

Mickey

A major drawback of MIKE was its command line orientation and its limited range of interactive techniques. In particular, it would not do the kinds of user interfaces that one finds on the Apple Macintosh and similar systems. In response to these difficulties, Mickey was developed to explore the language UIMS paradigm in the context of direct manipulation interfaces.

User Interface Specification

Rather than use a separate interface editor, Mickey extracts its user interface specification directly from the Pascal code. The presentation issues are handled by the Macintosh resource editor.

As with many other UIMSs, Mickey views the application as a set of services that are to be made available interactively. In Mickey this set of services is defined as a Pascal Unit, which is a separately compilable module. Mickey parses the interface portion of such a unit to extract the necessary information about the application's interactive services. The interface portion of a Pascal Unit provides sufficient information to access that unit interactively, but it does not provide information for menu placement, external names, function key equivalence, or other interactive presentation information. In order to supply this presentation information, any symbol declared in the interface unit can have a set of properties associated with it. These properties are specified using the (* *) form for Pascal comments. The following fragment of an interface unit illustrates the use of property comments.

```
UNIT SimpleDraw;
INTERFACE
  USES MickeyServe, MKW, DrawUtil;
  PROCEDURE NewDrawing (
    (* Menu=File Name='New...' Key=N*)
      DrawFile : OutFileDesc);
  PROCEDURE OpenDrawing (
```

```
        (* Menu=File Name='Open...' Key=O*)
        DrawFile : InFileDesc);
```
IMPLEMENTATION

    . . . .

END.

The NewDrawing procedure declaration is augmented by the property list
(* Menu=File Name='New...' Key=N*) which states that NewDrawing is to be
invoked from the File menu using an external name of New... or the
command key N. Other than the mappings between interactive techniques
and various Pascal constructs, the only other syntax that an interface
implementor must learn is to associate property lists with symbols.

Macintosh/Pascal Mapping

The interface specification is guided by a mapping between the declarative
constructs of Pascal and the interactive techniques of the Macintosh. The
key idea is to use basic concepts for modeling information and actions
which have been developed in computer science. Programming language
designs have provided constructs that support such modeling. Similar
constructs that accomplish similar goals are also found in user interface
design. The differences lie in the transitory nature of user interfaces, as
opposed to the specification nature of programming, and in the visual
nature of user interfaces. It is the similarities, however, that Mickey
exploits in its dialog model. The remainder of this section illustrates the
relationships between Pascal constructs and their interactive corollaries.

Commands/Procedures

The simplest relationship is the one developed in EZWin and MIKE. This is
the relationship between a procedure and an interactive command. The
following is an example of a Mickey specification of a menu of commands.

```
        PROCEDURE NewDrawing ( (* Menu=File Name='New...' Key=N *)
        DrawFile : OutFileDesc);
        PROCEDURE OpenDrawing ( (* Menu=File Name='Open...' Key=O *)
        DrawFile : InFileDesc);
        PROCEDURE CloseDrawing; (* Menu=File Name=Close Key=W *)
        PROCEDURE SaveDrawing; (* Menu=File Name=Save Key=S *)
        PROCEDURE SaveDrawingAs ( (* Menu=File Name='Save As...' *)
        DrawFile : OutFileDesc);
```

Based on these procedure definitions and their specified properties,
Mickey generates the following menu.

    As a command is selected, Mickey prompts for the command's

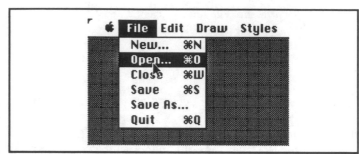

arguments. As with MIKE and EZWin a set of argument types provides basic interactive techniques.

Point input a 2D geometric point
RubberLine input the end points of a line using a rubber-band line
RubberRect input the corners of a rectangle using a rubber rectangle
InFileDesc select a file to be read using the standard Macintosh dialog
OutFileDesc specify an output file using the standard Macintosh dialog

Shared Menu Variables

The real contribution of Mickey comes in the notion of shared variables. Variables that are declared in the interface unit are considered to be shared between the application and the user interface. The user's interaction with these variables depends on the variable's type declaration and its specified properties.

The following is a sample Macintosh menu for setting text and drawing style information.

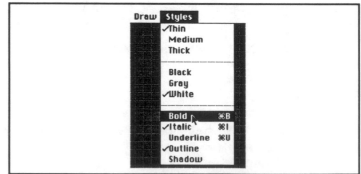

Fig. 8:8
Sample
Macintosh
Menu

This menu is created by the following Pascal declarations:

```
TYPE
    LineWidth = (ThinLine (*Name=Thin *),
             MedLine (*Name=Medium*),
             ThickLine (*Name = Thick *) );
    FillColor = (BlackFill (*Name=Black*),
             GrayFill(*Name=Gray*),
             WhiteFill (*Name=White*) );
VAR
    LineSize (* Menu=Styles *): LineWidth;
    ColorSetting (* Menu=Styles *): FillColor;
VAR
    BoldText (* Menu=Styles Name=Bold Key=B*) : Boolean;
    ItalicText (* Menu=Styles Name=Italic Key=I*) : Boolean;
    UnderLineText (* Menu=Styles Name=Underline Key=U*) : Boolean;
    OutlineText (* Menu=Styles Name=Outline *) : Boolean;
    ShadowText (* Menu=Styles Name=Shadow *) : Boolean;
```

Since the variables LineSize and ColorSetting are defined as enumerated types they are represented in the menu as check lists. For example, selecting Medium from the menu causes the variable LineSize to be set to MedLine. LineSize is a variable in the interface unit which can then be freely accessed by the application code. The BoldText variable is declared as Boolean and thus becomes a checked item in the menu. Selecting Bold from the menu sets BoldText to True and marks Bold with a check mark. Selecting Bold again sets it to false and removes the check mark. Toggled items, which switch between two settings, are specified using enumerations with only two choices, as in the case of the GridSetting variable shown below.

```
TYPE Gridding = (
        GridOn (* Name = 'Turn Grid On' *),
        GridOff (* Name = 'Turn Grid Off'*) );
VAR   GridSetting (* Menu = Draw *) : Gridding;
```

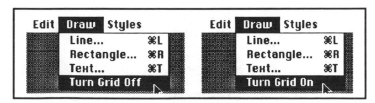

Fig. 8:9
GridSetting

Dialog Boxes

For variables that are more complicated than simple selections, a variable
with a Record data type can be used. When a dialog item is selected from
the menu, its corresponding dialog box appears with the current values
for that variable in the dialog fields. The user then interacts with the box
in the standard way. Selecting OK sets the variable that corresponds to
the dialog box; selecting Cancel (or the close box) removes the box
without modifying the variable. The following StyleOfText variable is an
example of this

```
TYPE   Str40 = STRING[40]
       TextStyle = RECORD
           Font : Str40;
           Points (*Name='Point Size'*) : Integer;
       END;

VAR    StyleOfText(*Menu=Styles Name='Text Style...'*): TextStyle;
```

Fig. 8:10
StyleOfText

Each type of field has its own kind of dialog item. Fields that are
themselves records can be used, which will cause a nested dialog to be
created within the main dialog box. The following example shows how
enumerated types would be handled.

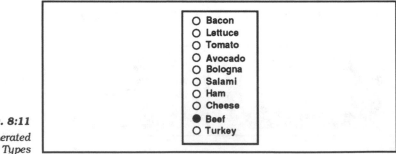

Fig. 8:11
Enumerated Types

```
Type SandwichItems = (Bacon, Lettuce, Tomato, Avocado, Bologna,
           Salami, Ham, Cheese, Beef, Turkey);
     Sandwich = Record
        Items: SandwichItems;
     End;
```

Guards

A UIMS must allow the application to verify that certain changes are
appropriate and to, possibly, take action when a change is made. Mickey
handles this with a Guard property that can be associated with variables
and fields. The guard property is a procedure that is called to verify that a
change is appropriate. Before making a change to a variable value, the
guard is invoked with the new and old values. The guard procedure can
perform any operations in response to the change and must return True or
False to verify the change. Returning False will cause Mickey to disallow
the change and will warn the user.

Application Windows

The language/user interface mapping breaks down when it comes to the
windows that the application actually draws in. In these cases Mickey
allows the specification of routines to be called for the various events that
can occur. In this area it offers nothing more than the event handler
UIMSs described earlier.

Dialog Management Algorithm

The algorithm for managing the dialog is very similar to that used in MIKE,
except that the full expression syntax is not possible and there is no
command line. All of the information describing the procedures, variables,
and data types is generated as Macintosh resources and is used by
Mickey's run time routines to control the dialog. Macintosh resources are
generated for the menu and dialog boxes. These resources can be edited
by the Macintosh resource editor to improve the presentation. Special
resources are also created which map menu and dialog items to their
appropriate interactive and semantic behaviors.

Summary

The UIMSs described in this section have moved to a higher level of user
interface specification than simply drawing the screen or handling the
input events. These models have used programming language constructs
as a basis for an overall interactive environment. There are trade-offs in

this approach. Because of its programming language orientation this system has proven to be very easy for programmers to learn to use. Because the UIMSs starts to dictate a standard interface model they are much less flexible that the other approaches. These UIMSs will not create all possible interfaces. They enforce their own style.

These models are targeted specifically for application analysts because they are driven by the semantic definition of the interface. Having defined such semantics, the user interface is derived immediately. MIKE's profile editor allowed graphics designers to become involved in the interface design without requiring a programmer. Both EZWin and Mickey required programmer intervention to define their presentation information.

The dialog specification is almost nonexistent in this model. The acquire and release operations are handled automatically by the argument type information. MIKE and Mickey provided specific routines which could enable and disable semantic commands if needed.

References

1 Lieberman, H. *There's More to Menu Systems than Meets the Screen*. **Computer Graphics** 19(3): 181-89, July 1985.

2 Olsen, D.R. *MIKE : The Menu Interaction Kontrol Environment*. **ACM Transactions on Graphics** 5(4): 318-44, October 1986.

3 Olsen, D.R. *A Programming Language Basis for User Interface Management*. **Human Factors in Computing Systems (CHI '89),** April 1989, 171-76.

4 Olsen, D.R. and J.R. Dance. *Macros by Example in a Graphical UIMS*. **IEEE Computer Graphics and Applications** 8(1): 68-78, January 1988.

9.
Constraint Systems for Visual Presentation

Most of the systems discussed so far have focused on the input side of dialog management, with little attention being paid to the visual aspect of dialog management. The visual portion of a graphical dialog has three parts: 1) the specification of the visual appearance including colors, patterns shapes, and placement; 2) the specification of the relationship between the visual appearance and the input; and 3) the specification of the relationship between the application data and the visual appearance.

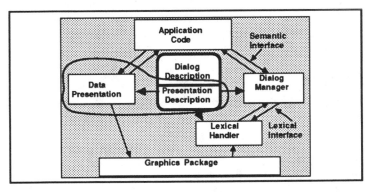

Fig. 9:1

These three specifications are a major part of the presentation description. The algorithms that operate on these specifications are the core of the data presentation component.

The input/visual and data/visual relationships are particularly important when creating direct manipulation interfaces. If the "feel" of direct manipulation is to be maintained, then moving the mouse or twisting a dial must create the corresponding change in the image in real time. In addition, changing the image must also change the underlying information that the image is presenting. Conversely, when application data changes, a corresponding change must be made in the visual image.

Thus we have two problems: 1) to find an appropriate representation for the data/visual and input/visual relationships, and 2) to develope algorithms efficient enough to maintain these relationships at interactive speeds. One promising approach is the use of constraint systems. A constraint system consists of a set of equations that defines relationships between values in the application, visual images, and input devices. Solving systems of constraint equations and interactively specifying the appropriate equations for a particular interactive task is the subject of the remainder of this chapter. The specification of constraints by graphics artists and dialog authors is a particularly thorny issue.

The discussion will be in three parts: 1) the general principles of constraint systems; 2) the major algorithms for solving them; and 3) examples of UIMS work which have applied constraint systems to the design of the visual portions of user interfaces.

Overview of Constraint Systems

Constraint systems are characterized by the types of equations allowed in constraints, the kinds of changes to the constraint system allowed at run time, and the algorithms used to solve the constraints. The types of equations allowed in a constraint system have a lot to do with how the algorithms can solve the system.

Constraint Equations

All constraint systems view the properties of the visuals, the inputs, and the application data as variables in a system of equations. For example, consider the following diagram system of equations.

> Mouse location
>   MouseX, MouseY
> Application data
>   ScrollMax, ScrollMin, Current
> Visuals
>   Top, Bottom, SliderCenter

$$\frac{ScrollMax - ScrollMin}{Top - Bottom} = \frac{Current - ScrollMin}{SliderCenter - Bottom}$$

> MouseY = SliderCenter

The preceding set of variables and the two equations form a simplified definition of a scroll bar. What is desired is that during dragging (change in MouseY) the scroll bar center should move (and be updated) while the Current value in the application is changed in a corresponding way. If,

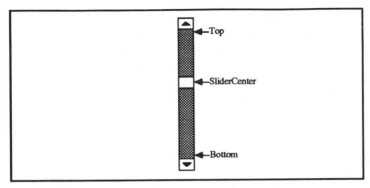

Fig. 9:2
Scroll Bar

however, some search command wants to assert a new Current value, the mouse location is irrelevant but the ScrollCenter and the part of the image that it controls must be updated to maintain the constraints. The constraint system shown above only establishes a relationship between the variables. Which variables are held constant and which can change, in a given situation, remains to be specified. The virtue of constraint systems is that they establish such relationships, which can be maintained automatically by the UIMS throughout the interaction.

One-way Constraints

One-way constraints are the simplest form of constraint system. They are closely related to the attribute grammars used in compiler construction.[1] All constraint equations are of the form:

$$D = F(I_1, I_2, \ldots I_j)$$

where F is any function of the independent variables $I_1 \ldots I_j$. Whenever the values of the independent variables change, the value of the function must be recomputed and assigned to the dependent variable D. If D is used in any other function, then that function must also be recomputed and so forth.

An example of such a system would be the following, which ties the mouse to a graphical slider value (between 0 and 1) and then ties the slider value to the rotation angle for some object on the screen.

$$CurrentSliderVal = \frac{(MouseY - Bottom)}{(Top - Bottom)}$$

$$XRotation = CurrentSliderVal * 360$$

One-way constraints are easy to handle: the dependent variable can only be set after the values of the independent variables are all known.

Two-way Linear

Although one-way constraints work for linking inputs to visuals, there are problems when they are used to link application information to visuals. When tying inputs to visuals the changes to the input should change the visuals, but the visuals have no need to change the input. When tying visuals to the application the relationship should be at least two-way and, possibly, multi-way. When an input changes the visual presentation, perhaps by dragging, the corresponding application data must be changed. When the application data are changed, the corresponding visual information must change.

The easiest class of equations to use are the linear equations, since solving for any variable, and solving simultaneous constraints, is very straightforward. The slider is an example of such a constraint system using the equation:

$$\frac{\text{ScrollMax} - \text{ScrollMin}}{\text{Top} - \text{Bottom}} = \frac{\text{Current} - \text{ScrollMin}}{\text{SliderCenter} - \text{Bottom}}$$

which can be converted to linear form.

Two problems arise when Current changes. These are: 1) which of the other variables should be held constant, and, 2) which variable should be solved for? There are various methods for resolving these issues.

The easiest method is simply to state that everything is constant except for Current and SliderCenter. When Current changes, then SliderCenter should be solved for and vice versa. This establishes a two-way relationship between a geometric entity and an application value.

The simple linear mapping will break down if the size of the slider changes (as is the case of window scroll bars when the window is resized) or if the ScrollMax or ScrollMin values change (as is the case when the size of a list being scrolled through changes length). The simple linear map can be written as:

$$\text{SliderCenter} = A * \text{Current} + B$$

where

$$A = \frac{\text{Top} - \text{Bottom}}{\text{ScrollMax} - \text{ScrollMin}}$$

$$B = \text{Bottom} - \frac{\text{ScrollMin}(\text{Top} - \text{Bottom})}{\text{ScrollMax} - \text{ScrollMin}}$$

The values of A and B are determined by one-way constraints. Once they are known the relationship between SliderCenter and Current is a two-way linear relationship. If any variable other than SliderCenter is changed, then SliderCenter is solved for, as in the case of one-way constraints. If SliderCenter is changed then Current is solved for. Note that in this form the definitions of A and B need not be linear since they are essentially one-way constraints.

Simultaneous and Non-linear

The two forms discussed so far have required that the constraints not be systems of simultaneous equations; that is, the solution to each constraint was resolved independently of other constraints. We have assumed that we consider each equation on its own and that at the time when we consider the equation there is only one unknown variable. In the case of our two-way constraints we have insisted on linear equations. The following dial is an example of a system where this does not work.

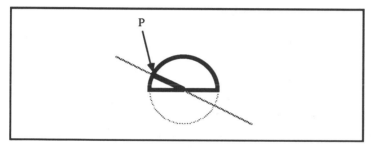

Fig. 9:3

The position of point P is determined by the equation of the line that defines the dial's wiper and by a distance from the center. The location of P requires the solution of two equations (line and distance) and two unknowns (Px, Py). In addition, one of these equations (distance) is quadratic.

Issues in Solving Constraints

There are four major issues to be considered when solving constraints: 1) specifying what has changed and what is being held constant; 2) planning the solution so as to minimize run-time cost; 3) structuring the constraints both for ease in specification and use and also for ease in finding solutions; and 4) determining whether a system is over or under constrained.

What has Changed?

The issue of what has changed is an important one. In many constraint systems, changes are modeled as removing and adding constraint equations. In other systems, the constraint equations have not changed, only the values of certain known variables.

Given our basic slider constraint:

$$\frac{\text{ScrollMax} - \text{ScrollMin}}{\text{Top} - \text{Bottom}} = \frac{\text{Current} - \text{ScrollMin}}{\text{SliderCenter} - \text{Bottom}}$$

we see one equation with six unknowns. If the mouse has moved the slider center, we would then add the constraint:

> SliderCenter = MouseY
> *where MouseY is a known constant from the input*

We now have two equations and six unknowns which does not have a unique solution. We could add

> ScrollMax = previous ScrollMax
> ScrollMin = previous ScrollMin
> Top = previous Top
> Bottom = previous Bottom

where all of the previous values are constants. This gives us six equations with six unknowns and a unique solution.

Many constraint systems simplify this view by marking variables as known or unknown rather than adding constraint equations for the known variables. In this view there is one constraint equation.

$$\frac{\text{ScrollMax} - \text{ScrollMin}}{\text{Top} - \text{Bottom}} = \frac{\text{Current} - \text{ScrollMin}}{\text{SliderCenter} - \text{Bottom}}$$

one input variable (SliderCenter), and four frozen variables (ScrollMax, ScrollMin, Top, and Bottom).

The issues of what has changed, what is frozen, and what are the base constraint equations are very important in planning solutions to a constraint system. Many constraint systems offer *incremental* solutions where knowledge about what has changed since the last solution is used to minimize the cost of computing the new solution.

Planning

Many constraint systems rely on planning algorithms to guide their solutions. In many cases the planning algorithms are run at design or compile time to produce ordinary sequential solutions that can be executed at run time. Constraint solution planning has two main processes.

First, the order of the constraints must be considered. In the case of one-way constraints, the constraints must be ordered so that all argument values are known before the dependent variable of a constraint can be computed. Such planning is the purpose of the attribute propagation algorithms used in compiler construction.[2] Secondly, the selection of functions must be considered. In one-way constraints the function selection is already done by the nature of the constraint definition. In multi-way constraints the variable to be solved for must be selected and a solution function for that variable must be derived from the constraint equation. A particularly knotty problem involves constraints that have multiple roots, as in the case of quadratic constraints.

Structuring Constraints

So far we have discussed simple constraint systems where all of the variables and all of the constraints are lumped together. In a real interface with hundreds of variables and constraint equations such a structure is inefficient and unmanageable. Consequently, various structures have been imposed on constraint systems to get control of both the computational complexity and the understandability of large constraint systems.

The simplest structuring system (frequently used in graphics) is that of rectangle, region, or window hierarchies. At the top level is a window, screen, or other global rectangle. Each rectangular region can have zero or more subregions. Each subregion has its position defined relative to its parent region, and possibly its sibling regions. For example, take the following layout.

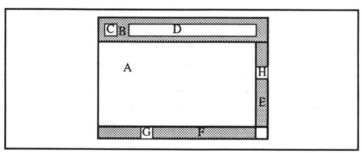

Fig. 9:4
Screen Layout

This is actually a tree of window regions.

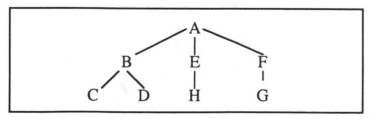

Fig. 9:5

The placement of D, for example, could be defined as centered vertically within its parent region. D's left edge might be a fixed distance from the right edge of C, with its right edge being a fixed distance from the right edge of its parent. Some systems use one-way constraints that depend only on the dimensions and position of the parent window. Such top-down approaches are useful then the user has control of the size of the top window and everything inside must adjust to the user's wishes. In other cases the size of a window might depend on the space needed to display its contents or to accommodate all of its subregions. Such a bottom-up approach may conflict with overall screen size or the amount of space that a user wants to give to a window.

In either the top down or bottom-up approach, the constraints are structured within regions. Each constraint system defines the geometric relationships between the subregions of a given region and relative to the parent region. The only communication between these systems of constraints is the positioning of intermediate regions. For example, the constraint system of A would only affect, or be affected by, H because the constraints involving A and H can both reference the edge positions of E.

The X toolkit does not use constraints for these problems but instead contains a geometry manager.[3] The geometry manager functions by widgets making space requests from parent widgets which then make determinations about their child widgets. A process of negotiation then resolves any differences.

In rectangle hierarchies the only communication through the hierarchy of constraints is by setting the positions of bounding rectangles. Attribute hierarchies are somewhat more general in that an arbitrary number of variables (or attributes) can be shared between a parent constraint system and one of its subsystems. An example of this is the Juno system[4] which uses hierarchies to control the complexity of its constraint solver. In Juno all variables are two-dimensional points. One might define a constraint system that controls the shape of the letter A.

When the A is defined, two of its points are defined as external points.

When the A is used in a larger system, only the two external points are visible to the larger constraint system. The constraint solver first solves the larger system, then the constraint system for each instance of A is solved using the external points fixed at the positions found in the higher system. A given system can have any number of external points. The example shows that shared variables are not limited to the bounding edges of an object.

Juno uses a numeric process to solve each level of the constraint hierarchy. When systems of one-way constraints are used, the technology of attribute grammars can be applied.

Attribute hierarchies use trees as their structuring mechanism. At least one system has been proposed that uses arbitrary graphs as the structuring mechanism.[5] The use of graphs rather than trees can move information directly to where it is used rather than requiring its propagation up the hierarchy to a common ancestor and then back down a different branch.

Over Constrained and Under Constrained

If a constraint system has more equations than it has unknowns, it is said to be over constrained and may not have a solution. If a system has more unknowns than it has equations, then it is under constrained and may have an infinite number of solutions. A system with an equal number of constraints and unknowns (properly constrained) may still not have a solution (parallel lines) or may have more than one solution (quadratic equations). Usually a properly constrained system will have a finite number of solutions. Equations involving trigonometric equations can have an infinite number of solutions. However, solutions outside the 0 to 2π range are discarded.

Constraint solution systems have varying ways of dealing with over and under constrained systems, as well as of dealing with multiple solutions. If a system is over constrained, then the additional (and hopefully redundant) constraints can be treated as tests to be checked at run time. In many cases the additional constraints may help to eliminate some of the multiple roots. If a system is under constrained, then some of the remaining unknowns may be fixed at their previous values until enough unknowns are eliminated so as to arrive at a properly constrained system.

General Planning and Evaluation Algorithms

The primary cost of using constraint systems in user interfaces is in solving the system of constraints. Even with linear systems of constraints the solution is $O(N^3)$, where N is the number of constraint equations. In order to alleviate this cost, algorithms have been developed for preplanning the solution so that most of the cost is borne at interface design time rather than when running the interface. The planning and evaluation algorithms are especially simple for one-way constraints. The two most common multi-way algorithms are propagation of known states[6] and propagation of degrees of freedom. In the case of a properly constrained system each of these will yield similar results. They differ when the system is over constrained or under constrained. Neither algorithm works for a constraint system that requires solutions of simultaneous equations.

One-way Planning and Evaluation Algorithms

The basic rule for evaluating one-way constraint systems is that a constraint can be evaluated whenever all of its independent variables are known. Because the constraints are one-way, only one evaluation sequence need be computed for the constraint system. The algorithm for planning an evaluation sequence is as follows:

```
Mark all variables that appear as dependent variables as unknown
Mark all other variables as known
ConstraintList := the list of all constraints
SolutionList := Nil
Done := False;
While not Done Do
   {If a constraint C is found in ConstraintList for which
        all independent variables are known then
     Mark the dependent variable as known
     Add C to the end of SolutionList
     Remove C from ConstraintList
   Else
     Done := True;
   }
```

The resulting topological sort will guarantee that each constraint appears in the SolutionList after all of its independent variables have been computed.

Once a constraint system has been evaluated, it is frequently the case that only a few of the variables are changed at a time. It is desirable to reevaluate only what is necessary, rather than reevaluate the entire constraint system. One such algorithm is the triggered incremental update algorithm.

```
For each variable V keep a list (Uses(V)) of all constraints where
   that variable appears as an independent variable.
Change( V,NewVal )
  { V:=NewVal
  For each constraint C in Uses( V )
    { Tmp := Recompute C
    Change( C.DependentVariable, Tmp )
    }
  }
```

This is a very simple algorithm; it recomputes only those constraints that
need to be recomputed. However, a given constraint may be recomputed
more than once. Take, for example, the following constraint system.

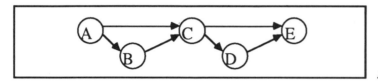

Fig. 9:7

B = F(A)
C = G(A,B)
D = F(C)
E = G(C, D)

Using our update algorithm for changing A, the following might occur.

Change(A) causes recompute of C
Change(C) causes recompute of E
Change(C) causes recompute of D
Change(D) causes recompute of E *2nd time*
Change(A) causes recompute of B
Change(B) causes recompute of C *2nd time*
Change(C) causes recompute of E *3rd time*
Change(C) causes recompute of D *2nd time*
Change(D) causes recompute of E *4th time*

The problem lies in the fact that when a variable is recomputed it is only
known that something has changed; it is not known whether more than
one thing has changed and whether the constraint should wait until all of
its independent variables have been updated.

The marked incremental update algorithm ensures that each
constraint is evaluated only once for each change of attributes.

Assume that all variables are marked as known and have computed
values
For all variables V that have changed
  PropagateUnknown(V)
For all variables V that have changed
  PropagateKnown(V)

PropagateUnknown(V)
  {if V is marked known then
    { Mark V as unknown
    For each constraint C in Uses(V) Do
      PropagateUnknown(C.DependentVariable)
    }
  else
    *ignore since unknown has already been
      propagated*
  }

PropagateKnown(V)
  { Mark V as known
  For each constraint C in Uses(V) Do
    if all independent variables of C are known then
      { Evaluate C
      PropagateKnown(C.DependentVariable)
      }
  }

The algorithm works by first propagating through the system the full
extent of what will be changed. The dependents of each variable are visited
once at the most, and, because any subsequent visits will find the variable
already marked as unknown, the algorithm will not follow its
dependencies a second time. Once all potential changes are marked as
unknown the actual changes can be calculated. Repeated calculations are
avoided since no constraint is evaluated until all of the changed
independent variables have been recalculated.

Propagation of Known States

In propagation of known states we start with the variables whose values
are known and search for variables that can then be solved for. When we
find new variables to solve for, they become known and new solutions
become possible. The algorithm is as follows:

```
Mark all input variables and frozen variables as known
Mark all other variables as unknown
SolutionList := nil
ConstraintList := a list of all constraint equations in the system
Done := False;
While not Done Do
    { Search ConstraintList for a constraint C
      which has only one unknown variable V
    If C is found then
        Create an assignment of the form
            V = F( . . . . . )
            where V is the unknown variable and
            F is produced by solving C for V
        Add the assignment to the end of SolutionList
        Remove C from ConstraintList
        Mark V as known
    else
        Done :=True
    }
```

At the end of the algorithm, SolutionList contains a sequence of functions and assignments which, when executed from beginning to end, will produce a solution to the constraint system. The solution list can be evaluated in time $O(N)$. The solution list is, however, dependent upon which variables are initially marked as known. For example, in the case of a mouse input, the mouse location would be marked as known, and possibly several other variables. The geometric location and the application information could then be solved and a solution list generated which could be used each time a new mouse input arrives. The same set of constraints could produce a different solution list if the application data were marked as known. In this case the solution list would work from the changed data to produce new geometric locations that are consistent with the constraints. The value of constraint systems is that the same, consistent set of constraint equations governs the relationships. Different solution lists are generated for each of the various situations.

Propagation of Degrees of Freedom

The propagation of degrees of freedom algorithm works by starting from variables that can be determined in only one way. In this algorithm we look for a variable that is controlled by only one equation and assume that that equation must be solved for that variable. The solved equation is then removed and the process repeated. This algorithm assumes that the freezing of a variable, or its use as an input, will be represented by that variable appearing in an equation $V = C$, where C is a constant. The algorithm is as follows:

```
Done:=False
ConstraintList := List of all constraint equations
SolutionList := Nil
While not Done Do
   { Find a variable V that occurs in only
        one member C of ConstraintList
    If C is found Then
      {Create an assignment of the form
        V = F( . . . . . )
       where V is the unknown variable and
       F is produced by solving C for V
      Add the assignment to the beginning of SolutionList
      Remove C from ConstraintList
      }
    else Done := True;
   }
```

The solution list will again contain a sequence of function evaluations which will solve the constraint system.

Freezing Assumptions

As mentioned earlier, constraint systems must determine what is known and what can vary. The standard propagation of known states algorithm assumes that all variables to be held constant have been explicitly identified as known. In the case of our slider example the constraint defines a mapping between the SliderCenter and the CurrentValue. Freezing all of the variables is a hassle for the interface designer. The interface designer would like to specify that SliderCenter has changed (marked known) and then have the system automatically determine that CurrentValue should be solved.

Our formulation of two-way linear constraints provides some help in this area. Remember that each constraint is of the form $Y = aX + b$. We can refer to Y as the dependent variable, X as the independent variable, and a and b as the control variables. If we were to leave the control variables unfrozen and freeze either X or Y with a constant equation, then the propagation of degrees of freedom algorithm might select one of the control variables to solve for. We can modify the algorithm so that when it selects variables to solve for, it puts dependent variables as the highest priority, independent variables next, and then control variables. Note that whether a variable is dependent, independent, or control is not a property of the variable but a property of its use in a particular constraint.

Assigning priorities to variables works for constraint systems other than the two-way linear. The specification of such priorities can, however, have nonintuitive effects on the resulting solution.

The freezing assumption problem can be handled in the propagation of known states algorithm by assuming that all control variables are already known. In this approach, whenever the independent or dependent variable becomes known, the other can be solved for. This simplistic solution will fail if the control variables are themselves the dependent or independent variables of other constraints. This problem is remedied by assuming that control variables that appear in only one constraint are known. Control variables that appear in other constraints would then have their known states propagate as before.

Iterative

The final general approach to solving constraints uses iterative numeric solution techniques to solve simultaneous constraints. The nature of the various approaches will not be discussed here since in most cases they are too inefficient for interactive use.

User Interface Visual Presentations

The preceding section discussed various forms of constraint systems and the general algorithms for solving them. The overall purpose for presenting constraint systems was as a mechanism for handling the visual presentation aspects of user interface design. In looking at each of these following uses of constraint systems the issues will revolve around: 1) how visual presentations are created, 2) what kinds of constraints are used with them, 3) how the designer specifies the constraints, and 4) how frozen or constant variables are identified.

Fixed Visuals

One of the earliest design tools for visual interfaces was MENULAY.[7] The metaphor was simple. A designer drew a picture of what the interface should look like. Icons were fixed in position or were moved explicitly by the application code. There were no provisions for presentation of application data.

Systems like the Apple Macintosh provide resource editors for defining

---

the visual presentation of an application. Such resources are data objects that contain descriptive information about the menu text, highlighting of menu items, and the geometric layout of items in dialog boxes. Such definitions are however, static, in that they do not change at run time. Dynamic relationships, such as enlarging some items but not others when a dialogue box is stretched, must be provided by the application code. The resources only provide a starting point.

The visuals created by systems like Hypercard[8] have already been discussed. The metaphor is drawing static images with no dynamic constraints.

Two systems provide automatic generation of such visual presentations. In Mickey,[9] the record data types of the user interface are analyzed to create default dialog box layouts automatically. Menu structures are laid out according to the properties attached to commands and variables. The designer's control over this automatic layout is limited and the results are static in nature. For a more refined layout the Macintosh resource editor is used. The Chisel[10] system provides a more ambitious set of layout tools. The designer can specify preferences as to where items will be placed. Chisel attempts to satisfy these preferences in producing a layout. As with Mickey, however, the resulting layouts are static placements of the visual items.

Ordered Dynamic Rectangles

Several systems have provided visual interfaces to the specification of rectangular hierarchies of constraints. MIKE's[11] visual layout was defined as a tree of windows. Each window's position was defined relative to the borders of its parent window. Both the subwindows and the graphical primitives used a "dynamic coordinate" system. The X,Y components of a

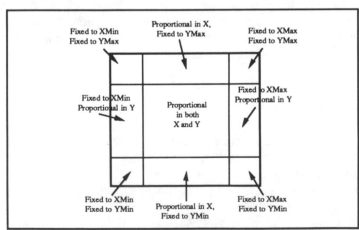

Fig. 9:8
MIKE

Constraint Systems for Visual Presentation

point were defined in one of three modes: 1) proportional distance between Max and Min, 2) constant distance from Min, and 3) constant distance from Max. The choice between the three forms is determined automatically based on where a point is specified. The following diagram shows the standard regions that MIKE uses to assign the form of the coordinates.

Objects drawn near the edges tend to stick to those edges while those drawn towards the middle are placed proportional distances between the edges.

A more flexible approach was developed by Luca Cardelli1.[12] A dialog in Cardelli's system is composed of rectangular *interactors*. Each interactor has an attachment point for each edge. These attachment points come in two forms. They are either proportionally spaced within the parent window, a constant distance from an edge of the parent window, or a constant distance from some other sibling interactor.

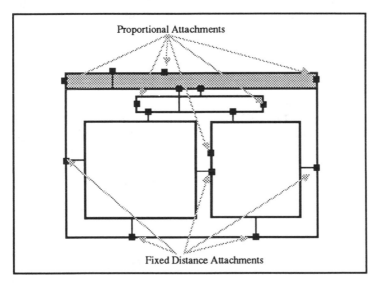

Proportional Attachments

Fixed Distance Attachments

Fig. 9:9
Cardelli

Cardelli's scheme allows more explicit control of the constraints as well as providing an explicit visual presentation of the constraints which allows for direct manipulation of the constraints by designers. An additional capability is that the constraints can reference each other to produce fixed size rather than proportional gaps between sibling objects. When interactors are first placed they are given proportional attachments. Double clicking on an attachment will attach it to the nearest edge of the parent, which in most cases is what is desired. Explicit dragging will form an attachment to a sibling.

A still more complex and more flexible approach is found in the Apogee user interface editor.[13] The basis for Apogee's placement of rectangular areas is reference lines. The two simplest reference lines are proportional and fixed.

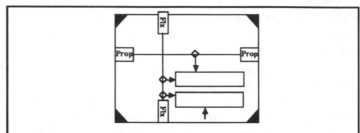

Fig. 9:10

Apogee

Reference lines belong to a containing rectangle. Fixed reference lines are located at a fixed distance from the edge of their container while proportional reference lines are at a proportional position. Once reference lines are placed, boxes can be placed either on a reference line or a fixed distance away. The arrows with diamonds at their bases represent fixed distance constraints from edges or reference lines.

Three innovative additions made by Apogee are the Max, Min, and general constraints. Max and Min constraints acquire their positions from the maximum or minimum positions of objects. The purpose of Max and Min is to allow the sizes of several objects to create a reference that other objects, or the outside edges, can align with. A general constraint is a reference line whose position is computed from some semantic expression.

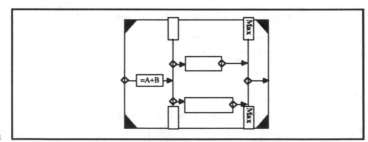

Fig. 9:11

Max and Min

In the example the left sides of both boxes are a fixed distance from a general reference line. The position of the general reference line is determined by the result of evaluating A+B. The positions of the right sides of the boxes are determined by the contents of the boxes. One might imagine that each box contains a string and that the sizes of the boxes are constrained by the lengths of the strings. The Max reference line is positioned a fixed distance from the longest of the two boxes. The Max reference specifies, in turn, where the right edge of the container box should go. Apogee is a much more flexible system for specifying visual constraints but there has been no experimentation as yet into how effectively interface designers can use this information.

All three of these systems use a system of one-way constraints. In MIKE the constraints are all calculated top-down from each window to its children windows. In Cardelli's system the sibling windows need to be ordered according to the algorithm described earlier so that the constraint dependencies between siblings are correct. Other than this sibling-ordering computations are top-down from the root window. Apogee seems to allow both top-down and bottom-up, but it is not clear what the evaluations sequence is for resolving the constraints at various levels.

Peridot

One of the more innovative systems for visually specifying graphical interactions is Peridot. Peridot stands for Programming by Example for Real-time Interface Design Obviating Typing.[14] As with the other systems in this section, Peridot's metaphor is one of drawing the interface. Peridot, however, is much more sophisticated in the depth of what can be expressed. In particular, it uses an inferencing mechanism for placing the constraints based on what the designer has drawn on the screen. This inferencing works not only for placement of single items but also for conditional and interactive placements. Peridot also allows the interactive mouse behaviors of visual objects to be defined by example.

Geometric Constraints

The placement of geometric constraints can be illustrated by an example. Suppose that the designer wants to create a pop-up menu box. The designer could begin by drawing a gray rectangle followed by a black rectangle.

Fig. 9:12

When the black rectangle is drawn Peridot runs through its set of rules looking for a rule that will hold between the black rectangle and the gray one. It takes each other graphical primitive (in this case there is only the gray rectangle) and checks it against each rule in the system. In this case a rule that checks to see if the two are close to the same size is found. Peridot also sees that the black rectangle is only a small offset from the gray one. When this rule succeeds, the designer is asked if the black rectangle should be the same size as the gray and should be offset by the number of pixels shown in the drawing. If the designer answers yes, then the appropriate two-way constraints are created to establish the relationship.

When a third white rectangle is drawn, Peridot detects that it is nested inside the black rectangle by a small amount that is close to the same on all sides. Peridot asks if the new rectangle is to be evenly nested inside the black rectangle. Again, if the designer approves then the appropriate constraints are created to derive the white rectangle's position from that of the black rectangle.

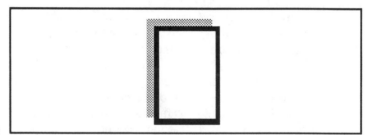

Fig. 9:13

The inferencing process is a simple one. Peridot has a list of rules. Each rule includes:

- the name of the rule
- a list of attributes that the rule will set
- a test to verify that the rule should be applied
- a message to ask the designer if the rule should be applied
- an action which establishes the constraint

When a graphical object is drawn or moved, then each rule is used to test the current object against all of the other objects. If the rule's test succeeds, then the message is sent to the designer for approval. If the designer approves, then the action is executed to set the constraint. The advantage of Peridot is that the designers need not remember all of the constraints that are possible. They simply draw what they want and

Peridot suggests constraints that will maintain that appearance. The designer need only approve the suggestions, without having to specify them completely.

The established constraints are two-way constraints. Initially, constraints are set so that the current object is dependent upon the other object that it is constrained to. In some cases, subsequent editing of objects may require that a constraint relationship be maintained but that the dependencies be reversed. This constraint reversal is handled automatically by Peridot, provided the designer first approves the change.

Inferencing Iterations

One of the innovative features of Peridot is its provision for iterative constructs. Given what has been drawn so far, we can also assume that

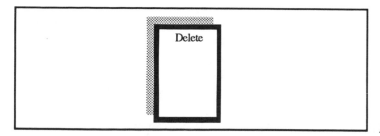

Fig. 9:14

the designer has specified that the object to be displayed is controlled by an active list of values.

(Delete Move Create Buy Sell Quit)

If the goal is to make a menu of these items, then the designer could select "Delete" from the list and place it in the drawing.

Peridot's rules see that the string is close to the top of the white rectangle and centered horizontally. If the designer approves these rules, the corresponding constraints are established. The designer might then select "Move" and place it centered under "Delete".

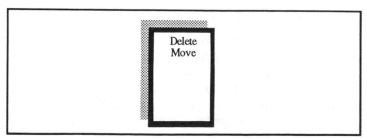

Fig. 9:15

Peridot detects the centering of "Move" relative to "Delete". When this rule is approved, Peridot also notices that the second element of this list has been placed relative to the first element. When successive elements of a list are constrained relative to each other, Peridot assumes that a loop is in order. It asks the designer if all elements of the list should be centered under each other. If the designer approves, then the result is as follows.

Fig. 9:16

This iterative inference has two advantages. First, it saves the designer the trouble of placing all of the items by hand and approving their constraints. Secondly, a general behavior has been inferred which can handle lists of any length.

If, at this point, the designer moves the bottom of the white rectangle to just under Quit, Peridot will ask if the bottom of the white rectangle should be constrained to the bottom of Quit. If the designer approves, Peridot notices that the bottom of the white rectangle is already constrained. It then asks for approval to reverse this constraint and those that depend on it. If approved, the bottom of the white rectangle is now dependent on the length of the list, the black rectangle is dependent on the white and the gray dependent on the black. This is the reverse of what was originally created and demonstrates the value of the two-way reversible constraints.

Mechanisms are also provided for creating conditional displays, such as highlighting objects if they are currently selected. The interface to conditionals is slightly more complicated than iterations.

Demonstrating Mouse Behavior

Peridot also provides a mechanism for specifying visual behavior in response to mouse input. This specification is done by demonstration. However, Peridot needs to know when a mouse input is part of Peridot's user interface and when it is part of the user interface being designed. Specifying mouse movement in the user interface being designed is done using a "pseudo mouse." The designer first specifies new graphics to be displayed as a result of mouse actions, such as graying a menu item when it is selected. The designer then drags the pseudo mouse to the desired location, sets or resets the mouse buttons on the back of the pseudo mouse, and selects the MOUSEDependent command. Peridot infers from the location of the pseudo mouse and the button icons that have been set the input conditions under which the demonstrated visual behavior should occur.

Other Drawing by Demonstration Systems

A similar system, which is not used for user interface design but which is used in drawing assistance, is Basil the turtle1.[15] The user works in a drawing environment using Basil the turtle to create things. When Basil thinks that he knows what the user will do next he tries to do it. The user can then approve or disapprove. The actions that Basil tries to learn are closely related to Peridot's iteration inferencing.

Simultaneous Constraints

The systems described so far handle one or two-way constraints. None of them handle simultaneous constraints.

Juno

The Juno system provides simultaneous geometric constraints. The constraints that Juno supports are the standard compass and straight edge constraints found in high school two-dimensional geometry. All drawings in Juno are defined in terms of points. The constraints are relationships between sets of two or four points.

(a, b) CONG (u, v): The distance between a and b equals the distance between u and v.

(a, b) PARA (u, v): The line from a to b is parallel to the line from u to v.

HOR(a, b): the Y components of a and b are equal.

VER(a, b): the X components of a and b are equal.

In addition to the above constraints, certain points can be frozen by placing a snowball icon on them.

Each of these constraints can be represented by an equation of degree two or less. The constraints are solved using a Newton-Raphson iteration technique. One of the problems that arises is that second degree equations can have two roots. Juno handles this by using the fact that iterative techniques tend to converge to the roots nearest their starting values. In cases where the user wants more control, hints can be added to the constraints to force particular starting values.

GITS

The iterative Newton-Raphson solution strategy is much too slow for use in interactive techniques. A system called GITS[16] provides solutions to these same sets of constraints by symbolically solving the constraints. GITS uses an editing model for its user interface. At the heart of the system is a drawing of an interactive technique. The technique is interactively manipulated by dragging portions of the drawing with the mouse. The constraints maintain the relationships between the drawing primitives, the semantic values of the application, and the mouse location.

When a designer creates an interactive technique with GITS six activities are involved.

1. Drawing the visual representation of the technique
2. Defining the semantic parameters of the technique (the data to be manipulated)
3. Placing constraints on the geometry of the drawing and between the geometry and the parameters
4. Defining the interactive operations to be performed on this technique such as dragging points or changing parameters and computing a constraint solution for each of them. These operations are referred to as methods
5. Defining methods which change application variables and computing solutions for these methods
6. Generating code

The horizon gauge in the diagram below illustrates a complex interactor for manipulating multiple parameters. This interactor manipulates both the roll and the climb from the same image. By dragging the small circle up and down the climb can be changed, and by dragging the wing line the roll can be changed.

Once a technique designer has drawn an interactive technique's visual representation the behavior of the drawing is specified by placing

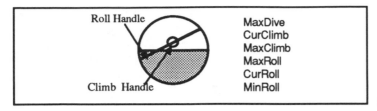

constraints on the points that define the drawing's geometry. Constraints are placed by selecting the kind of constraint desired from the menu and then indicating the geometric points or parameters that the constraint should reference.

There are two general classes of constraints. The geometric constraints control the relationships between points. The data mapping constraints control the relationships between the geometry and the semantic parameters.

Geometric Constraints

Horizontal (P1,P2)	P1.y = P2.y
Vertical (P1,P2)	P1.x = P2.x
Colinear(P1, P2, P3)	P1,P2 and P3 all lie on a straight line
Parallel(P1,P2,P3,P4)	The line P1,P2 is parallel to the line P3,P4
Congruent(P1, P2, P3,P4)	The distance from P1 to P2 is equal to the distance from P3 to P4.

Data Mapping Constraints

LProportion(P1,P2,P3, S1,S2,S3) *linear proportionality*

$$\frac{|P2-P1|}{|P3-P1|} = \frac{S2-S1}{S3-S1}$$

AProportion(P1,P2,P3,P4,S1,S2,S3) *angular proportionality*

$$\frac{angle(P1,P2,P3)}{angle(P1,P2,P4)} = \frac{S2-S1}{S3-S1}$$

The Horizontal, Vertical, Colinear, and Parallel constraints define lines that points must lie on. The Congruent constraint, which limits distances, defines circles that points must lie on. This means that all simultaneous geometric constraints in this system are solvable as intersections of lines and circles.

The data mapping constraints are the key to building interactive techniques. LProportion stipulates that P2 is the same proportional distance between P1 and P3 as the parameter value S2 is between S1 and

S3. If the parameters S1-3 are known and if any two of the points P1-3 are known, then the third point can be solved. If P1-3 are known and any two of the parameters S1-3 are known, then the third parameter can be solved. LProportion is used for such things as sliders or scroll bars.

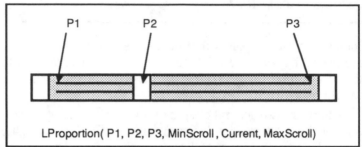

Fig. 9:19

LProportion(P1, P2, P3, MinScroll , Current, MaxScroll)

Angular proportionality constraints are used to define techniques like an interactive dial. Instead of mapping proportional distances this constraint maps proportional angles.

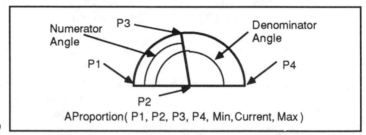

Fig. 9:20

AProportion(P1, P2, P3, P4, Min,Current, Max)

Given a drawing and a set of interactive constraints GITS allows the designers to specify interactive methods that can be performed on the system. Interactive methods are characterized by the kinds of things that can be changed; for example an application parameter or the interactive dragging of a point. The designer names a method and specifies the parameter or point to be changed. The designer then specifies all of the points and parameters to be frozen. A constraint solution is then requested. If the system is under constrained, GITS will indicate those variables that are still unknown and the designer can freeze some of them or add additional constraints. Over constrained conditions are also indicated.

Once all of the methods have been defined and valid constraint solutions computed, code can be generated for the interactive technique. This code is generated for a special object-oriented preprocessor to C. The interactive technique becomes a class, with each of the methods becoming methods of the class, and each method having code generated for it directly from that method's solution list. The generated code is linear in the number of constraints and graphical primitives.

GITS exploits the fact that there is a fixed set of constraints, all of which are either linear or quadratic. The GITS solver works by enumerating all possible combinations of the constraints. Since there are seven constraints there are 49 combinations of these constraints. In reality there are many more possible combinations of constraints. For example, two colinear constraints, each with three points, could share any combination of those points for a total of nine possibilities. Many of the constraint solutions, however, are symmetrical and there are actually less than 100 unique combinations of these seven constraints.

The solver works using a modified propagation of known states algorithm. As with the standard algorithm, GITS searches for constraints with only one unknown, adds a request to solve that one unknown to the solution list and marks it as known. When there are no remaining constraints with one unknown, GITS looks for pairs of constraints whose only unknowns are the (X,Y) coordinates of the same point. It then adds a request for simultaneous solution of the constraint pair to the solution list and marks both components of the shared point as known.

After the solution list has been generated and the system checked for over and under constrained conditions, the code generator can be run. It is the code generator that checks the symmetries of the constraint pairs and selects the appropriate solution macro invocation for generation. GITS then has solution macros hard coded for all of these combinations.

GITS does generate very fast code that completely integrates the application semantic values with a directly manipulated image. The largest problem with GITS is its handling of multiple roots. It has followed Juno's lead in selecting the solution closest to the previous solution. In the case of interactive dragging there is no problem since all movements are very small. In the case of parameter methods this approach can fail as shown in the figure below. When Current is changed from 2 to 8 the nearest solution to the pointer's end point is not appropriate.

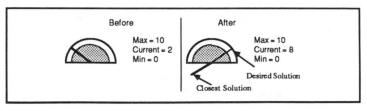

Fig. 9:21

Problems with Multiple Solutions

The multiple root problem can be resolved by placing restrictions on some of the constraints. Examples of such restrictions would be to require P2 of LProportion(P1,P2,P3) to lie between P1 and P3 or to require the numerator angle of AProportion to be smaller than the Denominator angle. Such restrictions were not included in the GITS prototype.

Summary

This chapter has discussed the need for tools to model dynamically changing visual images. Constraint equations are presented as a mechanism for establishing the relationships among images, inputs, and semantic values. These techniques apply almost entirely to the data presentation and dialog presentation portion of the UIMS architecture. The goal is that graphics designers can readily draw how the interface should look and then use constraints to attach the visuals to the inputs and to the application data. Several of the major constraint solution techniques were outlined. Problems still remain in the specification of constraints. Peridot has pushed this issue the farthest with its automatic inferencing of appropriate constraints, but more work is needed. The compass and straight edge set of constraints used in Juno and GITS are mathematically appropriate but are frequently not intuitive to designers.

References

1 Aho, A.V., R. Sethi, and J.D. Ullman. **Compilers: Principles, Techniques and Tools**. New York: Addison-Wesley, 1986, 279-342.

2 Demers, A., T. Reps, and T. Teitelbaum. *Incremental Evaluation for Attribute Grammars with Application to Syntax-directed Editors*. **8th Conference on Principles of Programming Languages**, January 1981, 105-16.

3 McCormack, J. and P. Asente. *Using the X Toolkit or How to Write a Widget*. **Proceedings USENIX Summer 1988 Conference**, 1988.

4 Nelson, G. *Juno, a Constraint-based Graphics System*. **Computer Graphics** 19(3): 235-43, July 1985.

5 Hudson, S. and R. King. *Semantic Feedback in the Higgens UIMS*. **IEEE Transactions on Software Engineering** 14(8): 1188-1206, August 1988.

6 Borning, A. *The Programming Language Aspects of ThingLab, a Constraint-Oriented Simulation Laboratory*. **ACM Transactions on Programming Languages and Systems** 3(4): 353-87, October 1981.

7 Buxton, W., M.R. Lamb, D. Sherman, and K.C. Smith. *Towards a Comprehensive User Interface Management System*. **Computer Graphics**, 17(3): 35-42, July 1983.

8 Goodman, D. **The Complete HyperCard Handbook**. New York: Bantam Books, September 1987.

9 Olsen, D.R. *A Programming Language Basis for User Interface Management*. **Human Factors in Computing Systems (CHI '89)**, April 1989, 171-76.

10 Singh, G. and M. Green. *Chisel: A System for Creating Highly Interactive Screen Layouts.* **ACM SIGGRAPH Symposium on User Interface Software and Technology**, November 1989, 86-94.

11 Olsen, D.R. *MIKE: The Menu Interaction Kontrol Environment.* **ACM Transactions on Graphics** 5(4): 318-44, October 1986.

12 Cardelli, L. *Building User Interfaces by Direct Manipulation.* **ACM SIGGRAPH Symposium on User Interface Software**, October 1988, 152-66.

13 Hudson, S.E. *Graphical Specification of Flexible User Interface Displays.* **ACM SIGGRAPH Symposium on User Interface Software and Technology**, November 1989, 105-14.

14 Myers, B.A. and W. Buxton. *Creating Highly Interactive and Graphical User Interfaces by Demonstration.* **Computer Graphics** 20(4): 249-58, August 1986.

15 Maulsby, D.L. and I. H. Witten. *Inducing Programs in a Direct-Manipulation Environment.* **Human Factors in Computing Systems (CHI '89)**, April 1989, 57-62.

16 Olsen, D.R. and K. Allan. *Creating Interactive Techniques by Symbolically Solving Geometric Constraints.* **Third Annual Symposium on User Interface Software and Technology**, October 1990, 102-07.

10.
Editing Dialog Models

As in the chapter on visual dialogs the systems described here are concerned with the problem of data presentation. In particular, they are concerned with how to integrate the presentation of the data with the interactive input. Early UIMS attempts concentrated almost exclusively on the input side of interaction and the handling of input events. The visual dialog systems were concerned with drawing visual portions of the presentation and with establishing relationships between the application data and the visual presentation.

The approach of the systems in this chapter is that the user interface should be determined by a model of the information to be interactively manipulated rather than by the commands that the user will issue. It can be asserted that most interaction consists of either browsing or editing information.[1] This is found to a limited extent in the transition from MIKE to Mickey, discussed in Chapter 8. MIKE was based exclusively on a model of the commands that were to be issued. Data types were represented only by names. In Mickey the type declaration information was used to create text edit boxes, dialog boxes, check boxes, and radio buttons. Each of these various interactive techniques is a form of editor for application data. An editing UIMS is driven by information about application data through the semantic interface and then provides interactive techniques for manipulating information.

An editor combines input handling and data presentation in a unified fragment of interaction. Take, for example, the simple text edit box. The model for a text edit box is that it is editing a string. Each of the user inputs has specific meaning for how the string is to be changed and is tightly integrated with how the string is to be displayed. Radio buttons and check boxes are similar editors for particular kinds of data. A dialog box is a mechanism for compositing editors together to form an editor for a composite piece of information.

Motivation for Data-based UIMS Models

Direct engagement with the information being manipulated is a major key in direct manipulation. In order for a UIMS to support direct engagement it must have a model of the information that it is manipulating. Early UIMS work only had a model of the commands and therefore the interfaces created by such systems were inherently indirect.

There are also a number of features a UIMS can support which are not possible without some model of the underlying application data. An undo facility must know about the application data so that it can put the data back the way they were before the changes to be undone were made. Many text editors and source code control systems provide facilities for managing patches, changes, or versions of text files. Similar facilities are of value in other interactive environments. A UIMS that understands the data that it is manipulating could support such features. Most graphical user interfaces do not provide search facilities. Again, if the UIMS understands the data model then the UIMS can provide such search facilities automatically. These are just a few examples of extended features that can be part of the UIMS and, therefore, be made available to all applications built using the UIMS. Such facilities require, however, that the UIMS knows about the application data.

Cousin

The Cousin system[2] was one of the earliest editing UIMSs. The heart of Cousin is the *environment*, which is a set of named and typed slots through that the interactive user can manipulate variables that communicate with the application. Entering parameters and commands is performed by editing the values in the slots.

The environment is controlled by a *system description* which specifies all of the information that Cousin needs about each slot. Each slot is described by:

- Name
- Data type
- Default value
- Constraints on legal values for the slot
- The syntax for values in the slot
- A textual description for explanations

For each data type Cousin provides an editor for manipulating the values of the slot.

Editing Templates

As the MIKE profile editor was being developed it was recognized that patterns of commands were being repeated over and over again. A list of menu items was manipulated in very much the same way as a list of windows, a list of data types, or a list of commands. All of the information about an application's user interface was stored in a system called STUF[3] (STrUctured Files). Essentially, this facility provided Pascal-style records and unions to be stored on disk files. The various kinds of lists were all stored in STUF structures as linked lists with a great deal of similarity between them. These similarities were exploited in a system called Editing Templates.[4]

An editing template is a particular kind of interactive editor which is parameterized in various ways to create particular application instances of the editor. An editor template has not only a particular interactive behavior but also a particular view of the data that it is editing.

A Linked List Editing Template

The linked list editor is an example of such a template. This template will scroll through a list of data objects that are stored in a linked list form. The parameters to this template would be:

> %ObjType — the STUF data type of the objects in the list
>
> %Link — the name of the field that is used to link successive objects together to form the linked list
>
> %CurIdx — this is a *cursor*, or a simple index to the current object tuple that is being edited.
>
> %HeadType — the STUF data type for the object that contains the pointer to the head of the linked list.
>
> %HeadField - the field in the header object that points to the first element in the list
>
> %XExt and %YExt — the X and Y extent of each element in the list's display.
>
> %Window — the window that the list is to be displayed in.
>
> %ObjDisp(Obj, X,Y) — an application routine which will display the Obj in the screen location specified by X and Y.
>
> %ObjDel(Obj) — an application routine to delete Obj.

The parameters represent the information that will tailor a generic linked list editor to a specific application. The linked list editor template would then supply the following command procedures which can be exposed directly to MIKE as part of the user interface.

%WindowUp — move %CurIdx up one item in the list. (Because of MIKE's command orientation all interfaces are key or event driven rather than direct manipulation. There are no scroll bars)

%WindowDown — move %CurIdx down one item.

%WindowLeft and %WindowRight — if the window is wide enough for multiple columns of items, this will move %CurIdx to the item immediately to the right or left of the current one.

%WindowPageUp and %WindowPageDown — moves %CurIdx up or down a full window's worth.

%WindowDelete — deletes the object referenced by %CurIdx.

In addition to the above command procedures there are several additional routines which can be used by the application code to interface with the generated instance of the template.

Restore%Window — will redraw the entire window by means of appropriate calls to %ObjDisp.

%WindowUpdateCur — will update the display of the current object in the event that changes have been made by the application.

%WindowInsert(Obj) — will insert the specified object into the linked list immediately after %CurIdx, make it the current object and update the display appropriately.

%WindowChangeCursor(Obj) — will make Obj the new current object in the list.

The editing template is primarily a piece of code that has been parameterized for a simple macro processor. In early versions of editing templates, a template user would supply values for each of the parameters and then run the template code through the macro processor to produce all of the code for a new instance of the linked list editor. The editor code would handle all of the editing and screen update issues for multiple column presentations of lists of anything. This provided a significant speedup in the creation of similar pieces of interaction. The routines shown above would all have application-specific text substituted for the parameter names (% —).

The application would then expose some of the routines directly to MIKE (as in the case of %WindowUp). The application could provide many other command procedures which would all work on the object referenced by %CurIdx. After changing the object they could invoke %WindowUpdateCur to get the screen updated. Insertion of new objects would be handled in this way since only the application would know how to create new objects of various kinds.

The linked list template is only an example. Several other editor templates were created. A simple extension to the linked list is the sorted linked list which uses an application-specific compare routine to determine if items are in sorted order. A tree editor provides for traversal and display of tree structured data. A schematic was created which provided editing facilities for nodes that were connected by arrows. The application data structures contain only the node and connection information, the editor provided all of the layout and maintained the node connections.

Architecture of Editing Templates

The original editing templates system consisted only of the code for each template, a set of parameters for each instance of the template, and the macro processor necessary to create an instance of the template from the parameters. This simple system was augmented by the creation of two special purpose applications (TED and ICE) which were built with the editing templates system.[5] Figure 10:1 shows the editing templates architecture.

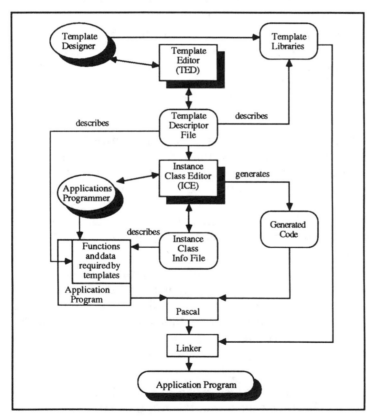

Fig. 10:1

Editing Templates

When one creates a new editing template, one builds a general library that will perform the desired editing functions. A template descriptor is also created which contains all of the information about how the template should be used. A template descriptor is created by TED (Template EDitor) and specifies the parameters to the template as well as the types that it uses, the application routines that it needs from the application, and the routines that the template will generate.

When an application programmer wants to use an editing template they use ICE (Instance Class Editor) to create a new instance class. An instance class is created when a template has parameters substituted into it. An instance class can then be used to create instances of the editor in multiple windows. For example, one could take the linked list editor template and describe it in a template descriptor. One could then create a student editor from the linked list template by supplying the information about linked lists of students. This student editor is an instance class. The student editor can then be used at run time to create instances of the editor in different windows for different lists of students.

Most of the code generated by ICE was to interface between the application and the generic code in the template libraries. This was particularly necessary because of Pascal's excessively restrictive mechanism for handling callback procedure addresses.

ITS

A more advanced model for editors is called Interactive Transaction Systems (ITS).[6] The semantic view of the ITS model is that a user is interactively editing information stored in tables. These tables are similar in nature to relational databases in that they contain tuples with fields of information and fields have types. The prime thrust of ITS development has been in abstracting the style (or presentation) of an interface from the rest of the dialog description and eliminating any syntactic specification issues by using an editing model for interaction.

This section will first discuss the four main components of ITS, followed by a deeper discussion of how dialog information is represented. The generation of a dialog specification tree will then be discussed in conjunction with the issue of style or presentation independence. Finally, some run-time issues will be covered.

Four Parts of ITS

The specification of an ITS dialog consists of a data definition, an interface content definition, style specification, and the run-time structures. All of these definitions are represented as trees of tagged items, each item having a number of attributes.

Data Definition

The data definition specifies the majority of the semantic interface to the application in the form of data and table definitions. For example:

```
:data type=fullname, structure=disjoint
  :di field=last, type=string
  :di field=middle, type=string
  :di field=first, type=string
:edata

:data type=student, structure=disjoint
  :di field=name, type=fullname, emphasis=special
  :di field=address, type=us_address
  :di field=parent, type=fullname
  :di field=class, type=integer
:edata

:table name=students
  :ti field=std, types=student
:etable
```

The purpose of the data definition is to specify the information to be interacted with. There are a variety of attributes that can be specified with each part of the data definition in order to provide information to the dialog about how this data is to be used and manipulated. Examples of such attributes are "structure=disjoint" and "emphasis=special." Such information is used by the views and the style rules to control the presentation.

Dialog Content

The purpose of the dialog content is to represent the logical (not presentational) form of the dialog and to specify the nonediting actions that the dialog is to take. The dialog content is specified at a relatively abstract level which consists of five basic components: lists, forms, choices, info, and frames. The dialog content specification is a neutral ground between the data definition and the style specifications.

A list is an arbitrary collection of things to be presented to the user, such as a list of all students or a list of files. All items in the list are assumed to be similar in structure and amenable to similar presentations for each element of the list. Note that the concept of a list does not specify how it is ordered, stored, or otherwise accessed (this is a data definition issue), nor does it specify how the list should be displayed (this is a style issue). The content specification simply indicates that a list of items should appear and specifies what information should appear. It is the business of the dialog content specification to indicate if all of the information about a student should be presented or only the name of the student. For example, a list of student names would be:

```
:list listname=student_names, table=students
  :li field=name
:elist
```

A form is a fixed collection of things. A form corresponds to a dialog box or property sheet. As with a list, a form would only specify what items are to appear in the form. The form would not specify how the items are to be displayed.

A choice represents a set of items from which a user must choose. Choices subsume constructs like buttons, menus, check boxes, and lists of check boxes. The dialog content specifies what the choices are, as well as what is to be done when a choice is made. A choice might be a choice of values such as:

```
:choice message="Class In School", field=class,
    kind=1_and_only_1
  :ci message="Freshman", value=1
  :ci message="Sophomore", value=2
  :ci message="Junior", value=3
  :ci message="Senior", value=4
  :ci message="Graduate", value=5
:echoice
```

A choice might also select among a list of actions to be taken. Such as:

```
:choice kind=1_and_only_1
  :ci message="Apply", action=Apply
  :ci message="Register", action=Register
  :ci message="Expel", action=Delete
:echoice
```

Info items are simply pieces of textual or graphical information that are to be presented to the user, such as help texts.

The dialog content is organized into a set of frames. A frame is a single conceptual unit of dialog. It would correspond to a top-level window on the Macintosh or in X. A frame is also analogous to a card or background in

HyperCard. It is a single, logical screen of information. An example frame might be:

```
:frame table=students
  :choice kind=1_and_only_1
    :ci message="Apply", action=Apply
    :ci message="Register", action=Register
    :ci message="Expel", action=Delete
  :echoice
  :list listname=student_names, table=students
    :li field=name
  :elist
:eframe
```

This frame would present a list of names of students and provide three possible actions to be taken on a student. The entire dialog content specification consists of a list of such frames.

Style Specification

The style specification is what controls the actual presentation of the user interface. The style specification is controlled by environments and rules. An environment is simply a named set of attribute values. Environments can also inherit attribute values from other environments.

The style rules are the key to the style independence of the dialogs. Style rules are basic if/then constructs. The if part specifies a pattern of attributes to which the rule will apply. The then part specifies an environment of attributes to inherit as well as additional units to be instantiated to flesh out the presentation.

Take, for example, the following two environments:

```
define text, view=string, font=times, size=10, justify=left
define special, parent=text, size=15
```

The following style rules could be defined

```
if (TAG=Form) & (Emphasis=special) Then (Match special)
if (type=string) then (Match text)
```

The rules and environments map special cases of the attributes into more extended attribute definitions. The idea is that issues of font size, color, font face, justification, line width, etc., should be specified relative to the abstract issues of what the item is for. A style then, is a mapping from the high level content specification to a particular presentation, as represented by the attribute settings.

The style rules are not limited to simple attribute settings. A style rule can also elaborate a particular item in the tree to a more complex structure. Take, for example, an item in a choice that has "kind=1_and_only_1." The style rule may want to specify that this be implemented as a radio button. To do this it must generate an item for the button and from the message attribute of the choice it must generate the label to go next to the button. The full scope of this rule language is beyond the scope of this discussion.

The most important attribute setting is the view. A view is a generalized editor that controls not only the presentation of the information but also how it responds to input events in manipulating the information.

Run Time

At run time all of the frames are represented as trees of views within ITS. These trees have had all of the style rules applied and are fully elaborated. When a frame is made active, its static representation is copied and the copy is decorated with appropriate information to tie its parts to the appropriate data instances. This forms the actual connection between the ITS dialog tree and the application data in the tables.

Generation of the View Tree

As has been mentioned, the run-time description consists of trees of views which handle the interaction between the user and the application. The key to ITS is in its generation of these trees from the various descriptions.

Mixing of Dialog Content with Data Definition

The first step is to use the data definition information to elaborate the content definition. In our example list only the field was specified for the elements of the list.

```
:list listname=student_names, table=students
  :li field=name
:elist
```

By searching the data definition we can elaborate this item with the type of the name field, which is "fullname," and the "emphasis=special" attribute. We can further elaborate this list item with a form that consists of the last, middle, and first name fields. The result might be:

```
:list listname=student_names, table=students
  :form field=name, type=fullname, emphasis=special
    :fi field=last, type=string
    :fi field=middle, type=string
    :fi field=first, type=string
  :eform
:elist
```

This dialog compilation phase fleshes out the dialog content specification by adding the additional information about the data being presented.

Mixing in of Style

The second step is style compilation. In this phase the style rules are applied to the new tree to add the necessary additional attributes. It is important to note that all elements of the tree inherit attributes from their ancestors in the tree. The fields in our example list would inherit the "emphasis=special" attribute. This would cause the "special" environment to be invoked which would decorate each of the fields with the attributes associated with special text.

Summary of ITS

ITS is based on a model of editing information. It has further refined the traditional UIMS model by factoring out the style rules. In essence, the style rules are those presentation specifications that are independent of a particular application. Mickey forms an instructive counterpoint to ITS.

Mickey used a semantic data definition which had similar content to that of ITS's data definition. The programmer, however, must explicitly control what is presented to the user interface, whereas in ITS the dialog content specification controls what is seen. The dialog compilation phase of ITS exploits the same semantic information that Mickey does in fleshing out the dialog definition. Mickey forces a particular style for presenting the abstract interaction defined by the semantics. ITS, however, has generalized these style issues in the form of style rules and environments rather than hard coding them into the system.

Sushi

Sushi (Raw Editable Objects) is a merge of the concepts found in editing templates and the architecture of Mickey. In Sushi the semantic model is specified by a set of object classes that are defined in COS (C Object System). COS is a C preprocessor which provides a simple class structure and message passing system and has the features needed to support

Sushi. It is possible that object-oriented languages such as C++ or Eiffel could support Sushi if modifications were made to the compiler to provide the needed information.

The interactive model is provided by *object editors*. An object editor is a COS class which is a subclass of ObjectEditor. User interfaces are built by combining application objects with editors appropriate to their class and then instantiating them on the screen.

COS

COS class descriptions are defined in a special language and then run through the generator to create C code for compilation and linking with the application program and Sushi. A COS class consists of a superclass and a list of methods and fields. The following are some example classes defined in COS.

```
Enumerated RegStatus Is {NotRegistered, Registered, OnHold}

Class Student Superclass Obj [ . . . ] {
    Data Field string Name;
    Data Field Address HomeAddr;
    Data Field Address SchoolAddr;
    Data Field Picture Photo;
    Method Field RegStatus Registration
        Read {* ... *}
        Write {* ... *};
    Method void Expel {* . . . *};
    Method void Hire( Wages )
        {* . . . *};
    }
Class Address Superclass Obj [ ... ] {
    Data Field string Street;
    Data Field string City;
    Data Field string State;
    Data Field long Zip;
    }
Class Wages Superclass Obj [...] {
    Data Field long Hours;
    Data Field long DollarsPerHour;
    }
```

Every class has a superclass and a set of fields and methods. COS defines both data fields and method fields. Normal methods also have their bodies programmed in C. A method in COS may or may not return a result, and may or may not have a single argument. If multiple values are needed as an argument they must be encapsulated in a COS object. This is somewhat awkward for programming but is natural for direct manipulation user interfaces.

A data field defines an actual field in the class's data definition and then defines two methods (for example Name and Name_) which will read and write that field. A method field, such as RegStatus, allows the programmer to code the read and write methods directly in C. This view of fields and methods allows a COS facade to be placed over any data model that the application programmers desire. The COS classes are only a user interface view of the application.

Aside from the generation of the C code to handle the class declarations and method invocation, COS also generates descriptive information for each class which provides two important capabilities.

1. A description of all methods with their names, argument, types, and result types.
2. A mechanism for formulating object messages at run time.

The class descriptor is attached to all COS objects and is used both by Sushi and by the underlying message-passing mechanism.

Object Editors

The key to Sushi's interactive behavior is the set of *editor classes* that it makes available. An editor class embodies a particular style for interacting with information. An editor class is refined or specialized by its *descriptor*. A descriptor is simply a COS object of whatever class is convenient for that class of editor. The descriptor for long integers, for example, would contain information about how many digits to allow, foreground color, text font, etc. A descriptor for a dialog box is more complex and contains information about where in the box the labels and subeditors should be placed. A descriptor contains information similar to the attributes in an ITS dialog tree. It is by editing descriptors that the interface designer can control the presentation aspects of the user interface. Since all descriptors are themselves objects, editors can be applied to these descriptors in the same way that any other portion of the user interface is defined.

When an editor class is combined with a particular descriptor an *editor* is formed. Every editor will edit objects of a specific class or any of its subclasses. An editor can be combined with an application object of the correct class and a window to form an editor instance. The role of an *editor instance* is to allow interactive users to browse, modify, and manipulate the application object according to the dialog specified by the combination of editor class and descriptor.

Editor classes generally come in two flavors: class-specific editors and composers. Class-specific editors always apply to a particular class of objects. The descriptor for a class-specific editor is only used to specify the presentation aspects of the editor. Composers are more general editor classes which can be specialized to a wide variety of object classes.

The editors and composers are stored in two lists which belong to the *editor environment object*. The prime purpose of the editor environment object is to maintain these two lists. The editor list contains editors whose descriptors have already been defined and specialized to a particular class. Editors are stored in the list by the name of the class that they edit and as a descriptive name. The descriptive name is important since more than one editor can exist for a given class of object. Composers are listed by name and type form (class, enumeration, union, or sequence) since they have not yet been specialized to a particular object class.

When an application exposes the editor environment object to the interactive user (by using an appropriate object editor for the environment object's class) the user or interface designer will have access to the editors and their descriptors. By selecting editors, editing their descriptors, or creating new editors from the composers, the interface can be interactively modified.

Object Class-specific Editors

The editors specific to particular classes include those defined on primitive types. There are editors provided for long integers, character strings, and Boolean values.

Supplying new class-specific editors is one of the easiest ways to extend Sushi. An example is an image editor. A COS class has been defined which provides access to images stored in a variety of formats with varying numbers of bits per pixel. Based on this class a special editor has been built and placed in the editor list under the BitMap class. Whenever BitMap objects are encountered, this special purpose editor is used. Other such special purpose editors have been built for color look up tables and color selection. The application programmer is completely free to extend this set.

Composers

A prime function of a composer is its GenerateDefaultDescriptor method which generates a default descriptor given a particular object class. As an example of how this works, consider the DialogBox editor class. Given the class of a particular object the dialog box editor would generate a default descriptor that provides a subeditor for each field in the class and a button for every method in the class. In the case of fields that themselves contain new objects, the default is to generate a button that will open a new editor on the object stored in that field.

The GenerateDefaultDescriptor method will only generate a default descriptor. Once a new editor has been created by generating the default descriptor, that descriptor can be edited to refine the editor. For example, many fields and methods might be removed from a dialog box to create a summary editor for that class. A new button could be added to the dialog box which would invoke the full editor on the same object.

The Application Programmer's View

As an example of how Sushi works we can trace through the process a programmer will take in developing a new application. Suppose that one wanted to build a simple application to store students with their pictures and mailing information.

COS

The first step would be to define COS classes for the information to be edited.

```
Enumerated RegStatus Is {NotRegistered, Registered, OnHold}

Class Student Superclass Obj [ . . . ] {
    Data Field string Name;
    Data Field Address HomeAddr;
    Data Field Address SchoolAddr;
    Data Field Picture Photo;
    Data Field RegStatus Registration;
    Method void Expel {* . . . *};
    Method void Hire( Wages )
       {* . . . *};
}

Class Address Superclass Obj [ ... ] {
    Data Field string Street;
    Data Field string City;
    Data Field string State;
    Data Field long Zip;
}
```

```
Class Wages Superclass Obj [...] {
  Data Field long Hours;
  Data Field long DollarsPerHour;
  }
Class Picture Superclass Obj [...] {
  Method Field long PixelIdx
    Read {* . . .*}
    Write {* . . . *};
  Method Field long CurPixel
    Read {* . . .*}
    Write {* . . . *};
  Method long Xdimension
    {* . . . *};
  Method long Ydimension
    {*. . . *};
  Method void ScanPicture
    {* . . . *};
  Private Field charPtr image;
  }
```

In the class Student, the Expel and Hire methods would have their implementations written in C by the application programmer. In the Picture class the fields PixelIdx and CurPixel would need their Read and Write methods written in C as well as the methods Xdimension, Ydimension, and ScanPicture. The ScanPicture method might run the scanner to enter a new picture.

The application programmer can create and manipulate objects of these classes by using the message-passing macros provided with COS.

EditObject

The programmer's primary interface with Sushi is via the EditObject routine. The programmer passes to EditObject the object that is to be shared with the user and the name of an editor to be used on that object. In addition, the programmer can84

indicate where on the screen the editor should be placed.

EditObject will take the class of the object and search the editor list in the environment object for an editor with the specified name and class. If such an editor is not found, EditObject will select an appropriate composer. EditObject makes a copy of the composer, sets its class name, and then invokes GenerateDefaultDescriptor to create a default descriptor for that class of object. This generation of default editors guarantees that an editor is always available for any class of object. Figures 10:2 and 10:3 show the editors automatically created for Student and Address.

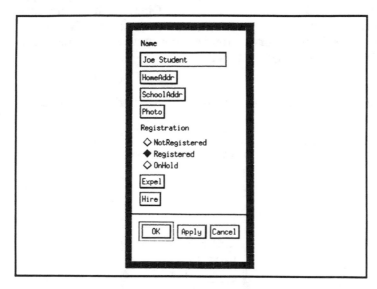

Fig. 10:2
*Default
Student Editor*

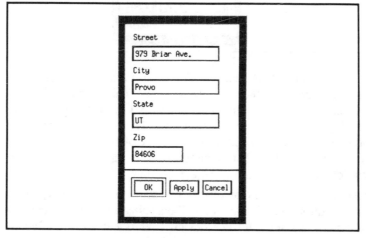

Fig. 10:3
*Default
Address Editor*

Once the new descriptor is generated the new editor is added to the editor list for future use. This eliminates regeneration of the same editor. This new editor is then copied again and instantiated by assigning it the object to be edited and invoking the editor's Create method. If an appropriate editor already exists in the editor list, then it is copied and instantiated with the object to be edited.

The programmer's view of Sushi can be summarized as: 1) create a semantic model as COS classes and 2) call EditObject to have the user interface objects displayed. Note that the programmer may only need to call EditObject once for a root or environment object which can then have subobjects which will cause new editors to open.

Adding New Editors

In the case of the Picture class the default generated editor would be as shown in figure 10:4.

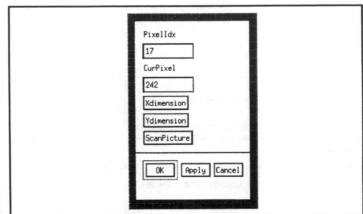

Fig. 10:4
*Default
Picture Editor*

This is not a useful interface to pictures. The programmer could take the COS class ObjectEditor and create a new subclass called PictureEditor. Inside the PictureEditor class the programmer would implement all of the methods necessary to edit pictures graphically. Having written this new editor class, the programmer would add an object of this editor class to the environment object's editor list. Whenever the programmer, or some editor, invokes EditObject on a Picture object, the new editor will be used.

Applications such as a paint program or a word processor frequently have some central editor that characterizes the application. Such a central editor will often need a user interface design that is carefully crafted to that application. The peripheral portions of the interface, like selecting colors, selecting fonts, or opening and closing files can be automatically supported by Sushi with little or no effort. Once that central editor has been created it is easily integrated into other applications that need to edit similar data.

Interface Designer's View

The interface design of a particular application is characterized by the editors in the editor list and each of their descriptor objects. By saving the class name and descriptor object of every editor one can completely capture the interface design. The application programmer can make the interface design available to users by calling EditObject on the editor environment object. The primary purpose of the editor for the editor environment object is to allow interface designers to: 1) create new editors from the composers; 2) copy existing editors to make new editors; or 3) modify existing editors by editing their descriptor objects. The editor for the editor environment object simply invokes EditObject on any descriptor object to allow interface designers to modify an editor. In their simplest form an editor for a descriptor may be a dialog box for setting fonts, patterns, or other resource type information. A descriptor editor may be a more complex editor like the one for dialog boxes, which allows designers to move subeditors, labels, and buttons around graphically as well as deleting subeditors and adding new ones from the editor list. Since descriptor objects are edited just like any other object, the interface design environment is just as extensible as any other part of the Sushi system.

Summary

In ITS editors (or views) are generalized by the use of numerous attributes that can be either specified directly or supplied by the environments and style rules. In X this same information is stored in resources. In Sushi this information is stored in descriptors but the descriptors are themselves editable objects. Sushi does have the capability of some style control in the use of the GenerateDefaultDescriptor message on composers. This is not as powerful, however, as the style rules of ITS. On the other hand, Sushi has a mechanism which neither X nor ITS directly support, which is the ability to apply its own interface model to itself in editing the descriptive information about the interface.

All of these systems support more of the data and dialog presentation parts of the UIMS architecture than the language and automata-based approaches. They accomplish this by explicitly representing the application information that is to be manipulated. None of these systems contain an explicit dialog specification. The dialog specification is implicitly derived from the combination of data to be edited with the selection of a particular editable presentation for that data. Systems like ITS and Cousin represent their presentations in a form suitable only for programmers or programming-oriented professionals. Although such presentation-based tools are the domain of the graphics designers the tools have not been geared to their particular skills. Sushi does allow the interactive editing of the interface in a way that a graphics designer could use. It suffers from the problem of each design being unique, whereas the style rules of ITS can be applied repeatedly to new applications. The extension of Sushi's GenerateDefaultDescriptor method to include ITS-like rules may provide the best of both worlds.

References

1 Olsen, D.R. *A Browse/Edit Model for User Interface Management.* **Graphics Interface '88**. Canadian Information Processing Society, June 1988.

2 Ball, E. and P. Hayes. *A Test-Bed for User Interface Designs.* **Human Factors in Computer Systems**, March 1982, 85-88.

3 Olsen, D.R. and R.P. Burton. *Structured Files for Interactive Graphics Programs.* **ISECON '88 Conference Proceedings**, 1988.

4 Olsen, D.R. *Editing Templates: A User Interface Generation Tool.* **IEEE Computer Graphics and Applications** 6(11), November 1986.

5 Blackham, G.D. **Editing Templates**. MS Thesis. Computer Science Department, Brigham Young University, Provo, Utah, 1986.

6 Wiecha, C., W. Bennett, S. Boies, J. Goold, and S. Greene. *ITS: A Tool for Rapidly Developing Interactive Applications.* **ACM Transactions on Information Systems** 8(3): 204-36, July 1990.

11.
Interface Quality

All of the previous chapters have concerned themselves with how user interface software is built and how the underlying algorithms work. There still remain the most important issues of "Is this user interface any good?" and "What might I do to make it better?" Since most user interface management systems maintain a dialog description, it has been hoped that automatically analyzing the dialog description as an aid in the interface evaluation process would be possible.

This chapter reviews three approaches to analyzing dialog information for the purpose of improving user interface designs. This chapter does not intend to cover the entire field of user interface evaluation. Instead it will show what has been done in exploiting machine-readable dialog descriptions for evaluation purposes. The first approach is use predictive measurement and analysis techniques. The second is one of automatically instrumenting the interface generated by the UIMS to collect measurements that can be mapped back to the original dialog description. The final approach is to define transformations on interface designs which preserve the semantics of the design while generating new design possibilities.

Predictive Analysis

The most attractive idea in evaluating interfaces is the concept of analyzing a user interface specification so as to point out problems or make predictions about how that interface will behave before it has been implemented. Obviously, if problems can be discovered before heavy implementation has begun, much time and effort can be saved.

Hand Analysis of Grammars

Reisner's early work on predictive analysis used formal grammars to represent the dialog description.[1,2] The grammar consists of the usual

---

terminals, nonterminals, and semantics described earlier in this book. In addition to these input-action symbols the model also contains *cognitive symbols*. The model is augmented by both cognitive terminals and cognitive nonterminals.

An input terminal consists of a single input to be received from the user. A cognitive terminal consists of a single information retrieval that must be performed by the user before proceeding. A cognitive nonterminal is simply mapped to phrases of smaller cognitive symbols. The purpose of these cognitive symbols is to represent the human mental activity necessary to operate an interface. The following is an example of how these symbols are used.

> <delete_line> ::= <c-find out how to delete line> <i-delete line>
>
> <c-find out how to delete line> ::=
>   <c-retrieve from human memory>
> | <c-retrieve from external source>
>
> <c-retrieve from human memory> ::=
>   <c-retrieve from long term memory>
> | <c-retrieve from short term memory>
> | <c-use muscle memory>
>
> <c-retrieve from external source> ::=
>   < c-retrieve from book>
> | <c-ask someone>
>
> <i-delete line> ::= *syntax for deleting a line*

Having created such a grammar for a user interface design the predictive process would consist of three parts.

1. Generation of sample sentences in the grammar.
2. Establishing cost relationships among the terminal symbols.
3. Analyzing the sample sentences.

The first step, generating sample sentences, consists of defining a benchmark task or set of tasks and then coming up with a sentence in the grammar that will accomplish those tasks. Here lies one of the major weaknesses of the approach in that there are multiple sentences capable of accomplishing a given task. Considerable judgement is required in the selection of such sentences, particularly in the selection of which cognitive symbols to use for a cognitive nonterminal. It is purely a judgement call as to how many times a user must ask someone for help before being able to remember the information. There is also the problem of the analyzer selecting a more optimal path through the grammar than a confused user would while stumbling through the interface. A similar problem is in not knowing the frequency with which various parts of the interface are used by real users and so have greater impact on performance and memory.

The second step consists of establishing relationships between the costs of the various terminal symbols. Actual cost numbers are not used in the analysis because of the extreme sensitivity of the process to the choice of these numbers. Instead, inequalities are defined, such as:

Time-for-long-term-memory > Time-for-short-term-memory

These inequalities are used in the analysis rather than actual data. This makes the system less sensitive to data values but does require a careful algebraic solution rather than a simple numerical one.

The last step of analyzing the sample sentences is used not to predict the performance of a given grammar but rather to compare the performances of two grammars. Two different designs are represented by two different grammars. Sample sentences are generated for both on the same tasks. The various kinds of terminals can be counted and comparisons drawn between the performance of the sample sentences.

Computer Analysis of Grammars

Bleser[3] extended the previous work somewhat by using multi-party grammars and automatic analysis. In particular her work focused on the use of input and output tokens in the grammar. The cognitive symbols described previously did not account for the user's response to what is happening on the screen. The key point of this work is the proposal of measurements and automated analysis of the grammar to aid in the evaluation.

Completeness

The completeness analysis simply reviewed the grammar to make sure that all nonterminals had been expanded, error conditions had been accounted for wherever they could occur, and all logical inputs had been assigned to input techniques and fully elaborated.

Consistence

The consistency analysis is based on a classification of the logical inputs such as attribute settings, commands, object selection, or output action. The set of classifications is an open one. The productions of the grammar are then analyzed to make sure that consistent ordering is used. For example, if most productions have a command token, followed by an object selection token, then any production with a differing order would be reported as potentially inconsistent. This type of automated analysis of large dialogues can be very useful.

Alternations

The last analysis is one of alternations, both physical and visual. A major design flaw in many user interfaces is that of requiring a user to switch between input devices. Many mouse-based interfaces require excessive movement back and forth from mouse to keyboard. The grammar can be analyzed for input sequences which have frequent alternations and problem areas can be indicated.

Similar analysis can be performed on output tokens. If each output token is annotated with information about where it is on the screen then sequences of output tokens can be analyzed to see if the attention of the user is focused in a particular area or forced to move around the screen for various icons, messages, or work areas.

Measurement of Implemented Interfaces

The previous discussion covered approaches for evaluating dialog specifications before they are implemented. A User Interface Management System also has several capabilities that provide unique advantages for measuring user behavior on already implemented applications.

1. A UIMS-based user interface can be rapidly modified by nonprogrammers.
2. Any capability added to a UIMS is automatically provided to all applications implemented with the UIMS.
3. The UIMS has control over all interactive input and output activity.
4. The UIMS has a separate description of the user interface which is not embedded in application code.

The rapid modification characteristics of UIMS-based applications have already been discussed. The second characteristic of amortizing UIMS capabilities over all applications is a powerful one. Any facility for measuring interactive user behavior that is incorporated into a UIMS is then available, without effort, in all user interfaces built with the UIMS. This eliminates the need for special logging facilities to be built into every application. The UIMS controls all interactive input and output and so the logging of interactive activity is relatively easy to add. With a hand-coded application such interactive activity is scattered throughout the code. This makes the addition and later removal of monitoring capabilities a time-consuming and error-prone task. The fact that a UIMS has a separate dialogue description is also of key importance. Whenever any interactive activity occurs, the UIMS knows exactly which portion of the interface description is in control and can charge that portion of the description with responsibility for that activity. This opens the crucial opportunity to map detected interface problems to specific areas of the user interface design.

It is very important to point out that measurements of performance times, number of keystrokes, or any other such metric can frequently leave interface designers in the dark. If, for example, a user is given a sample task and exhibits poor performance time on the task, the interface designer is still left with the question of what should be done about it. A good measurement tool must assign responsibility for behavior to particular portions of the interface design. In such a case the designer can then focus on those portions of the interface that exhibited the poorest performance rather than on the entire user interface. This ability to provide focused interactive usage measurements is an important aspect of the UIMS measurement approach.

Interactive Usage Metrics

Interactive usage metrics were added to the MIKE UIMS.[4] Having designed a user interface with MIKE and implemented its semantic routines one now has an interactive application ready for usage measurement. The new application is given to a sample set of users with a representative set of tasks to perform. As the users work with the interface MIKE's standard interface code will log the activity, along with identifying numbers for those commands and arguments that controlled the activity.

In developing this capability there was no attempt to invent new metrics. Metrics or characteristics identified by other researchers were used. Some user interface qualities, such as completeness and consistency described above, are already enforced by the UIMS itself. Others, such as user satisfaction, are too qualitative to derive directly from a log of user inputs. Some metrics, like learnability and retention,[5] could conceivably be deduced by studying changes in performance metrics over time. MIKE does not, however, provide such time-varying analyses.

As MIKE collects the metrics described below it will charge them to a particular command or argument of a command. All metrics are then reported by command and argument, which quickly leads the human factors expert to the source for detected problems. A review of the discussion of MIKE in Chapter 8 may be helpful in understanding the metrics described here.

Selection and Specification Effort

The need to map interactive behavior to the specification that controls it means that the metrics are separated into those controlling the selection of a command and those controlling the specification of a command. Selection activities include traversing the menu tree with mouse clicks, typing a command name abbreviation, or striking a function button. A simple selection metric might be the elapsed time between the prompt for the command and when the command is actually located.

Specification activities include entering the arguments for a command. Commands with no arguments, for example, would have zero specification time. In the case of commands used in argument expressions the selection phase of the command plus its specification would be charged in total to the argument itself and be charged against the specification of the command to which the argument belonged.

Take, for example, the following command expression:

CreateResistor((100,210), Multiply (100,63))

and the following list of events to invoke this command.

1. Select "Circuit Elements" menu item
2. Select "Capacitor" menu item
3. rub out
4. Select "Resistor" menu item
5. point at location (100,210) on the screen and hit the mouse button
6. Select "Arithmetic" menu item
7. Strike the "*" key
8. type in 100
9. type in 63

The interactive activity would be charged to the selection and specification of commands, and the specification of arguments in the following way:

Selection of CreateResistor	{ 1,2,3,4 }
Specification of CreateResistor	{ 5,6,7,8,9 }
Specification of the Location argument for CreateResistor	{ 5 }
Selection of Multiply	{ 6,7 }
Specification of Multiply	{ 8,9 }
Specification of Operand1 of Multiply	{ 8 }
Specification of Operand2 of Multiply	{ 9 }
Specification of Ohms argument of CreateResistor	{ 6,7,8,9 }

The reason for this separation of selection from specification is that there are two kinds of remedial actions to be taken. In the case of excessive time in selection, one might change the location of a command in the menu tree, change its command abbreviation, or attach it to an icon so that it can be selected rather than typed. In the case of excessive specification time one should consider rearranging the arguments or providing a more expressive set of functions for those argument values. It is most important that the metrics included in a UIMS reflect and highlight the dialog model of the UIMS. The metrics should lead an evaluator to specific parts of the dialog specification which can be modified to correct the problem that the evaluator has found. This requirement tends to make some of the metrics rather UIMS-specific.

General Metrics

There are four general metrics that apply to all commands and arguments. They are *performance time, mouse movement , command frequency,* and *command pair frequency.* Performance time has long been used as a user interface metric.[6-9] Mouse movement is not actual movement but the sum of the distance between mouse button hits. Poor mouse movement performance would lead one to rearrange the screen layouts or menu position to reduce unnecessary distances. Command frequency is useful not only when one wants to enhance performance of the most frequent cases but also when one wants to find which commands are completely unused. The frequencies of pairs of commands is an indication of how commands are used in combination with each other. Frequent command combinations should be placed logically and physically close to each other. If, for example, command A has a high selection cost and we find that it is frequently preceded by command B, which is in a different menu, then the recommendation would be to place A and B in the same menu.

Physical and Logical Inputs

A second set of metrics have to do with the actual input activity itself. Such metrics are divided into physical and logical input metrics. The physical metrics are the actual numbers of physical input events required to select or specify a command or argument value. This corresponds to the keystroke model of interface evaluation. In addition, by logging the number of logical inputs that have occurred in selection or specification other insights are obtained. If, for example, the number of logical inputs is high and the number of physical inputs is roughly the same, then the problem probably lies in the placement of the command in the menu tree which is causing excessive traversal effort. If, however, the number of logical inputs is low but the physical input count is high then the interactive technique for selecting the command should be changed by binding a function button to the command or shortening its abbreviation.

MIKE supports activities such as rub out, cancel, and undo as built in capabilities, so such activities can be counted and charged against commands and arguments. These counts indicate error rates. High rub out or cancel counts for a command would indicate that users are not understanding its function or are confusing it with another command. High undo rates would indicate that the user is using the command, not liking its result, and then recovering. Such measures could indirectly indicate confusion and learnability problems. These error metrics are differentiated between physical and logical inputs. Physical rub outs that occur while typing a string indicate typing errors while logical rub outs of command fragments indicate that the user has pursued a mistaken path.

Visual and Physical Alternation Costs

An interesting set of metrics are those that relate to visual and physical swapping. They were inspired by Bleser's work, described above. Physical device swapping measures the cost of switching between interactive devices in the course of selecting or specifying a command. Following this work a cost is attached to each such device transition (say from the mouse to the keyboard) and then these costs are summed for both selection and specification. This transition cost matrix can be altered by the human factors expert as will be shown later.

Bleser also suggested that the changes in the user's focus of attention on the screen should be measured. This is impossible to measure directly without eye-tracking equipment which most software developers do not have. MIKE's metrics are based on the assumption that any change on the screen represents a visual demand for the user's attention. To log all graphical activity would substantially slow down the graphics package, which could thus impact the validity of other measurements, and would produce massive amounts of data in the log files. These metrics are implemented by dividing the screen into a 4 x 4 grid of buckets and then logging which buckets the graphics package draws into in the course of executing a particular command. The 4 x 4 grid is used, instead of actual positions, to improve the performance of the logging software. The first metric charged to a command is the *actual output space*, or total number of buckets into which a command generates output. A second metric, the *output extent*, is the number of buckets in the rectangular extent which contains the actual output space. For example, in both figures 11:1a and 11:1b the actual output space is 2 but the output extent of figure 11:1a is 2 while the output extent of figure 11:1b (the gray region) is 6.

Another useful metric is the *dispersement ratio* which is defined as output extent divided by actual output space. In figure 11:1a the dispersement

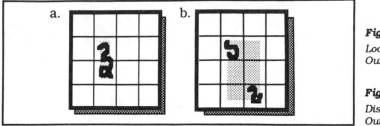

Fig. 11:1a
*Localized
Output*

Fig. 11:1b
*Dispersed
Output*

ratio is 1, but in 11:1b it is 3. Commands with high dispersement ratios are commands that do small amounts of output in widely separated portions of the screen. A rearrangement of the screen layout may resolve such problems. A very high output extent coupled with a dispersement ratio of 1 would indicate a command that is changing most of the screen. This would indicate a command that changes visual contexts. If context changing commands have a high frequency then possibly there are some design problems in the way contexts are used in the interface.[10]

Similar metrics to the three described above are derived by combining the graphical output locations with the mouse hit locations when marking buckets as used. These metrics help detect problems of long distances between where inputs are specified and where the output is being displayed. If one has a large screen with all of the menus located in the upper right hand corner of that screen then the combination of mouse movements and display would tend to produce a large dispersement ratio as mouse activity would tend to be remote from display activity.

Logging and Collecting Metrics

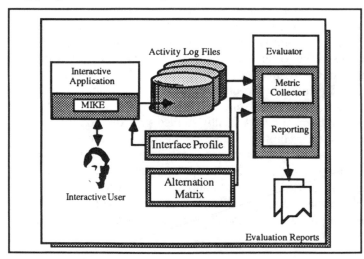

Fig. 11:2
*Metric
Collection
Architecture*

The architecture for collecting these metrics is shown in figure 11:2.

MIKE's standard user interface code was modified to log all physical and logical inputs along with the command and argument that they are to be charged against. In addition, MIKE notifies the graphics package to clear its visual output activity map just prior to the invocation of a semantic routine. When a semantic routine returns to MIKE, the map will be retrieved from the graphics package and logged against the command to provide information for the visual alternation metrics. The logs are written to files and then the files are read by the metric collector along with the matrix of alternation costs. This allows for multiple sessions to be logged and then later combined or analyzed separately. This also opens the possibility for new, more detailed analysis routines to be written to work from the raw data.

Once the logs have been generated by sample user activity, they are analyzed by the metric collection and report generation program. This program uses the Interface Profile to reinterpret the log and to generate human-readable reports about the interface. The metric collection routines use the device swap cost table supplied to it in generating the physical alternations metrics.

The Evaluation Process

A major problem with these metrics is the large amount of data produced. Example interfaces had over 150 commands with an average of 2 arguments per command. There are about 30 separate metrics generated for each command and its average two arguments, for a total of 13,500 data points. This is too much data for any human to make effective use of.

MIKE's approach was to take each metric one by one and to sort all commands (or arguments) in worst to best order relative to the selected metric and to report the commands in that order. Each metric has its own definition of what worst to best means. This is a simple technique for focusing attention where needed. This can be refined somewhat by specifying a limit for each metric on the number of commands actually printed. Thus one could request only the 10 worst commands for each metric and focus only on them. A facility is also provided for the human factors experts to specify composite metrics. In this case the sorted order for each metric is used to assign a rank to each command for each metric, with the highest rank being the worst relative to that metric. Use of rank numbers instead of metric values normalizes the metrics relative to each other. A weight can then be specified for each metric to be multiplied by a command's rank to produce a composite metric that can be used to print a sorted list of the commands. For more detailed analysis the metrics can be output in a form acceptable to most spreadsheet programs.

Usage Measurements in other UIMS Architectures

Most of the approaches implemented in MIKE can be transferred to other UIMS architectures. The two questions that arise are, 1) how can the basic information be logged, and 2) what units of the dialog specification should be charged with a particular action?

The allocation of interactive inputs to selection or specification effort is very much MIKE-dependent because this differentiation reflects the way in which MIKE dialogs are defined. Each UIMS would have its own unique differentiations based on the interaction styles and interactive techniques that it supports. The logging of performance times, physical events, and logical events should be easy in any UIMS that works from an input event queue. Planting logging calls in the routines that remove events from the queue would handle these input event metrics. The mouse movement and physical device alternation costs are handled by similar monitor probes. In fact, the basic logging capability is possible in any interactive application that uses such an event queue. The visual alternation metrics are slightly more difficult because probes must be placed in every graphics routine that writes to the screen. The command frequency and command pair frequency are more difficult in a UIMS which does not have a notion of the complete command. In grammar or transition diagram UIMSs it is difficult to differentiate between semantic calls that are performing simple echoing tasks and those that are real semantic operations. Additional information in the dialog specification could allow the dialog designers to make this differentiation between intrinsic semantic calls and mere feedback. The frequencies and pairings of intrinsic semantic calls would have more meaning than metrics on all semantics.

A more difficult problem encountered in grammar or transition diagram UIMSs is assignment of responsibility. One possible approach is to assign responsibility for metrics to the nonterminal or subdialog currently being processed. The problem with this is that on many occasions subdialogs or nonterminals must be introduced to handle anomalies in the UIMS's dialog control algorithm rather than for any intrinsic purpose of the user interface. Metrics on such nonterminals or subdialogs would distort their meaning. Again it would be possible to flag those units for which metrics would not be meaningful and charge their metrics against the units that called them. Another alternative is to charge all interactive behavior that occurs between calls on intrinsic semantic routines such as A and B as part of the interactive cost of invoking routine B. This has some problems because routine A may be preparing arguments for routine B. In the case of such a relationship the metrics associated with A should also be charged against B. In most UIMSs it is not obvious how one could automatically discover such a relationship.

Object-oriented and event-driven approaches to user interface development will also have some problems in assessing responsibility. The metrics can be collected, as before, in the graphics package and event queue handler. The problem arises from the absence of a centralized dialog specification. The specification of the dialog is distributed throughout the methods of the interactive objects. This distribution of function has several user interface design advantages but makes the responsibility assignment more difficult, if not impossible.

Transforming Interface Designs

One of the more innovative approaches to the issue of interface design improvement is the User Interface Design Environment (UIDE).[11,12] In UIDE the semantics of the interface are represented by the classes of objects that can be manipulated and the actions that can be performed on them.

IDL Descriptions of an Interface

The information about a class of interactive object consists of:

- the superclasses and subclasses
- the set of actions or methods on the object
- the set of attributes that an object can have.

Each action is characterized by the types of its arguments. This is similar in spirit to the semantic descriptions of Mike, Mickey, and Sushi, but is much richer in the kinds of information maintained. In addition to this descriptive information, each class contains formal statements about the initial values of its attributes. Each action has a formal statement about its preconditions and postconditions. For example, a CLOSE action on a FILE object has a precondition that the file is open and a postcondition that the file is closed. The purpose of the initial value assertions and the pre and postconditions is to allow the automatic design aids to reason about the interface and to make transformations on an interface design without violating constraints on the actions.

Transforming the Dialog Description

The heart of UIDE is a set of transformations that can be performed on a user interface without changing its semantics. The set of available transformations are:

1. create global (modal) attribute-setting commands,
2. create a currently selected object (object mode),
3. create a currently selected set of objects,
4. specialize a command,
5. create a currently selected command (command mode).

Before discussing these transformations it is useful to define a canonical form for actions. The canonical form is that all values required by an action be explicitly represented in the parameters of that action. For example, we think of a DrawLine action as having two end points as its parameters. In canonical form, the DrawLine action would be as follows:

DrawLine(p1:point, p2:point,
    pen:pattern, linewidth:integer, linestyle:arrow_style)

All of the information required to draw a line has been explicitly represented rather than implicitly retrieved from global variables. This allows the interface design tools to operate on all of the interface semantics rather than hiding some aspects.

The transformations are best described with examples. The factoring transformations take information out of a particular command's parameter list and place them in global variables with separate commands to manipulate the global settings.

In our DrawLine example we could factor pen, linewidth, and linestyle into global variables such as CurrentPen, CurrentWidth, and CurrentStyle. This is a type 1 transformation. We then generate special commands to set these global variables and replace DrawLine with a FactoredDrawLine which retrieves information from the global variables before invoking DrawLine. The FactoredDrawLine command will need additional preconditions stipulating that the global variables have been set.

Another example of factoring would occur when a line has several actions for changing its pen, linewidth, and linestyle. Each of these actions has the line and the new attribute value as objects. We can replace these by a SelectLine command which will select a line and make it the currently selected line. The SetLineStyle command would have the line object factored out of it as a parameter and would instead always apply itself to the currently selected line. This is a type 2 transformation. The

SetLineStyle command could be further modified to apply itself sequentially to all of a set of selected objects. This would require the creation of commands for selecting multiple lines and for adding lines to the selected set as well as removing them.

Let us also suppose that we are repeatedly changing lines into dotted lines. We could further transform the SetLineStyle command to a MakeDotted command which would set the linestyles of the currently selected lines to dotted. This is a type 4 transformation which substitutes specific values into a command rather than general parameters obtained from the user.

An alternative to creating a mechanism for selecting sets of lines is to use modal commands. We may make the SetLineStyle, SetLineWidth, and SetPen commands modal: that is, if any of these commands is selected then they are automatically applied to any line that is selected. This is a type 5 transformation. The pre and postconditions become very important here because SetLineWidth, and SetPen might be applicable to selected circles where SetLineStyle would not.

Each of the transformations described will substantially change the user interface behavior but will not affect the interface to the application in any way. This set of transformations provides a space of possibilities which can be explored with the help of the UIDE system. A major advantage of UIDE is that the transformations are easily requested and performed automatically, quickly, and correctly rather than manually, slowly, and with mistakes.

Evaluating Transformed User Interfaces

The evaluation metric that UIDE uses is the Keystroke Model.[13] The evaluation approach is based on obtaining a script of user behavior trying to accomplish a task. As a UIMS, UIDE has the same advantages that were exploited in MIKE; namely, the ability to semantically log everything that an interactive user does. When an interface generated by UIDE is used, the activity can be logged. From this log a Keystroke Model metric can be calculated as:

$$T(execute) = K(Keystroking) + P(Pointing\ at\ screen\ object) +$$
$$H(Homing\ on\ device) + D(Drawing) +$$
$$M(Mental\ Preparation) + R(System\ Response\ Time)$$

This metric is a predictor of user performance on the task. Let us suppose that an interface designer sees that users are repeatedly making lines with the same width, pen, and style. A factorization of these attributes can be proposed and the interface transformed. In addition to transforming the interface, UIDE can transform the script to a form consistent with the new interface. The keystroke metric can be applied to the new script to predict whether the new interface will enhance performance. Although UIDE only uses the keystroke metric in its prediction, most of the metrics used by MIKE would apply in the same way, since they are based on logs that are similar to UIDE's scripts.

In essence the UIDE approach provides the best of both worlds. Instead of relying on judgement calls or special hand calculations as in Reisner's work, the UIDE analysis uses actual scripts. Conversely, the MIKE metrics will point out what is wrong but will provide no information about how good particular solutions are until they are implemented and retried. UIDE, however, can use real scripts from actual usage to predict the viability of transformations of the interface.

There are some caveats in UIDE's evaluation approach. The first is that some transformations, such as using global settings instead of explicit values, may lead users towards very different patterns of usage from those in the script. These differences would reduce the accuracy of the prediction. In spite of these drawbacks the approach does, however, allow for rapid testing of new design alternatives with some quantitative feedback, which can help designers focus quickly on the alternatives that will be most fruitful for the next round of user testing.

Summary

In this chapter we have concentrated on the needs of the user interface evaluator. With predictive approaches an attempt to exploit the separate dialog descriptions that UIMSs provide is made. By analyzing the description before implementation it is hoped that poor choices can be avoided before their repair becomes expensive. All of the approaches discussed in this chapter rely heavily on the external dialog but the metric and transformation approaches also rely on a complete semantic definition. At present there are, however, no UIMS tools that analyze the presentation information. All of these approaches are hampered by the fact that a "good interface" is an ill-defined concept that depends greatly on the user's environment and background. These approaches can help in identifying problems and exploring alternatives but they are no substitute for the creative insights of a human designer.

References

1 Reisner, P. *Further Developments Toward Using Formal Grammar as a Design Tool.* **Proceedings of Human Factors in Computer Systems**, 1982.

2 Reisner, P. *Formal Grammar and Human Factors Design of an Interactive Graphics System.* **IEEE Transactions on Software Engineering**, 1981.

3 Bleser, T. and J.D. Foley. *Towards Specifying and Evaluating the Human Factors of User-Computer Interfaces.* **Proceedings of Human Factors in Computer Systems**, 1982.

4 Olsen, D.R. *MIKE: The Menu Interaction Kontrol Environment.* **ACM Transactions on Graphics** 5(4): 318-44, October 1986.

5 Shneiderman, B. **Designing the User Interface**. New York: Addision-Wesley, 1987.

6 Barber,R.E. and H.E. Lucas. *System Response Time, Operator Productivity and Job Satisfaction.* **Communications of the ACM** 26(11), November 1983.

7 Benbarat, I., A.S. Dexter, and P. S. Masulis. *An Experimental Study of the Human/Computer Interface.* **Communications of the ACM** 24(11), November 1981.

8 Card, S.K., T.P. Moran, and A. Newell. *The Keystroke Model for User Performance Time with Interactive Systems.* **Communications of the ACM** 23(7), July 1980.

9 Roberts, T.L. and T. P. Moran. *The Evaluation of Text Editors: Methodology and Empirical Results.* **Communications of the ACM** 26(4), April 1983.

10 Gaylin, K.B. *How are Windows Used? Some Notes on Creating an Empirically Based Windowing Benchmark Task.* **Human Factors in Computing Systems (CHI '86)**, April 1986.

11 Foley, J.D., W.C. Kim, and C.A. Gibbs. *Algorithms to Transform the Formal Specification of a User-Computer Interface.* **Interact '87**. Amsterdam: Elsevier Science Publishers, 1987.

12 Foley, J., C. Gibbs, W.C. Kim, and S. Kovacevic. *A Knowledge-based User Interface Management System.* **Human Factors in Computing Systems (CHI '88)**, 1988.

13 Card, S., T. Moran, and A. Newell. *The Keystroke-Level Model for User Performance Time with Interactive Systems.* **Communications of the ACM** 23(7), 1980.

Index

acknowledge...20
acquire 19-21,32,34,47,58,63,116,123-124,152
action expression(s) 41,142
active data...31
address 77
address table..28
aircraft 115
alternations...205
analysis...10
angular proportionality..178
Apogee 170-171
application 16,23,34-35,90
application analyst(s)...............................8,11-12,127,134,151
application interface model 4-5
application programmer(s)...9,11,28
Architectures...15
argument list...130
arguments 117,121,124,130
ASCII...18
attachment point...169
attribute grammars 49,155,161
attributes...24,50,52,69,71189
automatic analysis 205
automatic design aids 214
background..84
Basil the turtle 175
bit vector..108-109
Bleser..205,210
Boeing Computer Services..115
browsing 12

buttons..84,190
Buxton 73
C 24,26,28,77,178,193-195,198
C++ 194
CAD 115
call...41-42,52
callback(s) 27,83,188
cancel...143,210
canonical...215
Canvas 77
card..84
Cardelli..169
check box 190
Chisel...168
choice(s) 189-190
class..80
class declarations...195
class description(s) 194
class descriptor 195
class specific editors..196
cluster controller 96
clusters 96
cognitive symbols 205
cognitive terminals 204
color 82,153,191
command combinations 209
command frequency...209,213
command line...137,139
command model..23,25
command pair frequency...213
command procedures...23,24,185
communication 92,96
compiler construction...15,49,66,155
compiler theory 41
completeness..205
complexity..115
composer(s) 196,198,201
composite metrics 212
condition(s) 93,97-98,122
condition list 98
condition vector...102,104

conditional transition(s)..4,51
conflict 99
congruent...177
consistency..10,205
constraint systems 12,154
content definition 192
context 21,32,19,29,47,58,63,66
continuous input...22
control key 21
CORE 2,16,18,23,64
COS 193-194
Cousin..184,201
Data Display 31
Data Presentation..16
data..31
data definition 189,192
data display..28
data field(s) 194-195
data mapping constraints..177
data model 23-25
default descriptor 196
default dialog..139
defaults 119,121,125
delegation...79
demons 25
demonstrating mouse behavior 174
demonstration...145
descriptor objects 201
design 6
device independence...18
device swapping 210
dialog 6
dialog author(s)............................9,11-12,18,33,42,52,61,90,113,127,154
dialog box(es)..150,190,195
dialog content 189-190
dialog control 4-5,89
dialog description 3,9-10,24,26-29,31-35,38,52,58,90,203
dialog designer(s)..12,28
dialog evaluator..12,33
dialog handler 58
dialog manager....................5,16,18-19,21,23-24,26,31-35,38,40,127,130

dialog specification....................................4,7,12,127,129,136,137,188,201
dialog trees..12,115,122
direct manipulation 5,31,73,146,153,184,195
disable..20-21,32,34,41,58,62,66-67,97,99,104
dispersement ratio...210
distance...175
dragging 169
echo 20-21,139,141
editing...12
editing descriptors...195
editing dialog models...183
editing information 193
editing models...12
editing template 185-186
editing UIMS 184
EditObject 198
editor...195
editor class(es)...195-196,200
editor environment object...196,201
editor list(s) 198,200
Edmonds..37
Eiffel..194
enable.......20-21,23,32,34,40,56,58,62,66-67,97,99,104,116,117,124,126
End Users 8,134
English..85
Enter action 116-117
enumerated types...149
environment object..198
equations 154
error messages 32
error metrics 210
escape state(s)...52-53
evaluation 10,12
evaluation tools 7
Event Response Language...92
event(s)...18,21-23,93,96
event delegation..79,82
event device..18
event handlers..75
event procedure...77

event queue...23,29,32
event record 21,24
Execute action...117
Exit action..116
expressions 32
Extensibility..88
external control..3,75
external dialog description..38,75
EZWin...129
factoring transformations...215
Feldman...37
fields 24,84,98
flags 93-94
focus of attention..210
font face 191
font size...191
form(s)..189-190
formal language(s) 37,71
frame(s)..189-190
freezing assumption 166
frequency of pairs...209
frozen 158
function button 21
generated code 179
generated editor 200
generating code 176
geometry...175,176
geometry manager..160
GIGO...77
GITS...176
GKS...2,16,18,23,64
grammar 12,59,134,204
graphical editor 73
graphics artist(s)..4,154
graphics designer(s)...9,12,33,127,152
graphics package..18,35
graphs..161
GRINS 134
guard(s)..49-50,55-57,92,151
guard expressions 25
Hanau..59

help 32,52,204
highlight 20
HoldInput 38
human factors 11
human factors expert 207,210
HyperCard 73,84,168,191
HyperCard Event Handling 88
HyperCard inheritance 86
HyperTalk 85
icon(s) 21,32,34,82,167
implicit reject 120,125
incremental update 162-163
inferencing 171
inferencing iterations 173
information 183
inherit 97,193
inheritance 79-81,86-87,99,101,131
inherited attributes 49-50
input selector 42
inputs 12
Interactive Transaction Systems 188
interactive behavior 207
interactive methods 179
interactive object 76
interactor(s) 136,176
interface design 11,203
interface editor 136-137,139
interface evaluation 203
interface profile 136
internal control 3
internal description 39
internal dialog description 33,73
intersect 103
intersections 177
ITS 188,195,201
Jacob 37
Juno 160,175
justification 191
Kasik 116
keyboard 18
keystroke model 209,216

keystrokes 207
knob...18
language models..12
language processing 15,59
layout..34,142,168
learnability 210
Lenorovitz..59
leveled menus..122
Lexical Analyzer 21
lexical...15-16
lexical handler......................15,18,21,23-24,32,34,89,143
lexical interface 122-123
lexical level 132
light pen...64
line width 191
linear equations...155
linked list 186
Lisp 25,31,33,129
list editor..185
lists 189
LL(1)..61
local attributes 49
logging of interactive activity...205
logical device 16,18-19,21,32,40,47,67
logical events...213
logical pick device 65-66
MacApp..82
Macintosh 146-147,167,190
macro processor...186
macro(s) 11,145
Macros by Example 32
mask...109
measure 18,20
measurement(s)...10-11,32,203,205
measuring..10
measuring user behavior..206
memory...205
mental activity...204
menu 17,19-21,59,119,131,137,147,168,190,209
menu level...123
menu tree..119,208

MENULAY...73,75,84,143,167
message 80
message passing 198
method...80
method field(s)..194-195
metric(s) 207,209,212,216
Mickey..129,146,168,183
Microsoft Windows 79
MIKE 129,134,143,169,171,183,207,213
modifier keys...78
mouse 18,21-22,34
mouse movement 209
mouse movement events 22
movement number 116
multi-party grammars...205
multilayered menu 119
multiple root(s) 159,180
navigating 118
Newman..1,37
Newton-Raphson iteration...176
nonterminal(s) 41,49,60,66-67
NOW...42,57,95
NULL events 22
Object Pascal...82
object-oriented 25,32,73,79-80,87
objects..25
Olsen..37
one-way constraint systems 162
one-way constraints 155,171
output extent 210
output space 210
over constrained...178
overlay...103
parallel 175,177
parameter...24
partially independent 104
Pascal....................................26-27,59,134,136,146-147,185,188
password..55,57
patches 184
pattern 78,191
performance...205

performance time(s) 207,209,213
Peridot...171
personnel roles...8,11
pervasive state(s) 52,71
physical device 4,16,18-19
physical events...213
physical metrics 209
pick identifiers...65
picking 64,66
picking ambiguity..66
planning..162
planning solutions..158
portability...18
postconditions..214
PPS evaluation algorithm 102
preconditions 214
predict...216
predict performance 205
predictive evaluation 7
predictive measurement..203
predictor...216
prefix...139
presentation 4-5,7,15,138,145,188,195,201
presentation description..............................13,16-17,21,31-32,34,35,127
presentation objects 130
priorities...166
procedure(s) 24-25,136
production system(s) 97-98,113
productivity...10
profile editor 146,185
programming language..71,129
prompt 20-21,32,139,141,208
propagating..33
propagation of degrees of freedom 162,165
propagation of known states...162,165-166,179
property lists 147
property sheet 190
proportional distance 169
Propositional Production Systems 92,97
propositional logic 97
pseudo events 78,79

pseudo mouse 174
quadratic constraints 155
quadratic equations..161
query fields...100,104
Reaction Handler..1,37
recording:...145
records 24
recursive descent...66,69,71
recursive state machine(s)...36-37,41
redrawing 76
reenter..121
reenter state(s) 52,54
reference lines 170
regular languages..112
Reisner...203
relational databases 188
release..19-21,32,34,47,58,64
reliability 10
requirements..6
resource(s)..17,82-83,167,201
resource file..83
return 41-42
Rogers 37
rub out..66,71,143,210
rule elimination 110
rule indexing 111
rules...95,97-98,191
sample 21-23
sampled...18,22
sampled devices 16
SASSAFRAS 92,96,100
screen layout(s) 47,73,209
script..85
scroll bar..18-19,79-81
search 184
Seattle...2,5
Seeheim 4
select set 61
Semantic Interface 16,23,25,28,31-33
semantic(s) 15,23,25,55
semantic action(s)..............................12,27,32,34,60,75,77,99

semantic attributes 43
semantic command(s) 26-28,31
semantic conditions 97
semantic control..49,122
semantic data model 24
semantic expression..55
semantic field...100
semantic interface 4,6,11,24,28,34,65,127,136
semantic model 129
semantic procedures 24
semantic values...33
shared variables 148
shift key 78
simultaneous constraints...166
simultaneous equations 162
simultaneous solution...179
Sketchpad...1
software engineering...6,51
spatial demultiplexing 19,73
specification 7
stack...84
state diagrams...38,51
state machine 12,37,55,58,60,91,113,134
state space 97
state tables...40
STUF...185
style 188,191
style rules...189,192,193
style specification 191
subdialog...41
subset 102
SunView...77
super class...83
Sushi...193,196,201
SYNGRAPH 59,64-66,71,134
syntactic...15
syntax...94
synthesized attributes 49,50
temporal demultiplexing...19
terminals...60
Tiger...115

toolkit..27-28,77,82
tools 33
topological sort 162
transformations...215
transformations on interface designs............................203
transition cost matrix..210
transitions...34
translation table(s) 76,79,83-84,91
tree editor...187
trigger...18
trigonometric equations...161
type(s)..24,29,34,43,4,136,148,183
type checking 24
UIDE 214
under constrained 161
undo..145,184,210
UNIX 22
Unordered Inputs 91,94
usability 6,18
usage measurements...207
User Interface Design Environment 214
User Interface Evaluator...10
User Interface Management System 2
user interface design 6
user interface evaluation 203
user performance 216
users 8
variable(s)...148,151
versions...184
view..192
virtual device(s) 16-19
virtual world..9
visual alternation metrics...213
visual appearance 153
visual context..211
visual output activity..212
visual presentations 12
Wasserman 37
Widgets 82
window systems 75
window(s) 130,151,160,169

windowing package 27
windowing system(s).. 28,73
X 82,160,190,201
X-Windows 16,22,24,27,77
XCMD 88
YACC..59